ISBN 978-1-5283-1786-3
PIBN 10905777

1 MONTH OF
FREE
READING

at
www.ForgottenBooks.com

By purchasing this book you are eligible for one month membership to ForgottenBooks.com, giving you unlimited access to our entire collection of over 1,000,000 titles via our web site and mobile apps.

To claim your free month visit:
www.forgottenbooks.com/free905777

English
Français
Deutsche
Italiano
Español
Português

www.forgottenbooks.com

Mythology Photography **Fiction**
Fishing Christianity **Art** Cooking
Essays Buddhism Freemasonry
Medicine **Biology** Music **Ancient**
Egypt Evolution Carpentry Physics
Dance Geology **Mathematics** Fitness
Shakespeare **Folklore** Yoga Marketing
Confidence Immortality Biographies
Poetry **Psychology** Witchcraft
Electronics Chemistry History **Law**
Accounting **Philosophy** Anthropology
Alchemy Drama Quantum Mechanics
Atheism Sexual Health **Ancient History**
Entrepreneurship Languages Sport
Paleontology Needlework Islam
Metaphysics Investment Archaeology
Parenting Statistics Criminology
Motivational

THE
C. M. TRAVER CO.
New York

COLLECTION OF
RARE AMERICAN
ANTIQUES

IMPORTANT CARVED CHEST ON STAND
AMERICAN, 17TH CENTURY

[NUMBER 315]

RARE HOOKED RUGS
WITH A FEW RARE PIECES FROM

MISS TRAVER'S
PRIVATE COLLECTION

OUND BY

OUND BY

[282]   [138]   [318]   [302]   [307]   [313]   [109] [321]

A ROOM AT THE CARNEGIE INSTITUTE, PITTSBURGH, PA., SHOWING A NUMBER OF RARE PIECES
LOANED BY MISS TRAVER FOR AN EXHIBITION OF AMERICAN PERIOD FURNITURE, 1922
THE OBJECTS NUMBERED APPEAR IN THIS CATALOGUE

SALE NUMBER 1952
PUBLIC EXHIBITION FROM THURSDAY, APRIL NINTH

THE

C. M. TRAVER CO.
New York

COLLECTION OF

RARE AMERICAN ANTIQUES

COMPRISING

IMPORTANT SEVENTEENTH CENTURY PIECES
KNOWN TO COLLECTORS AND LISTED IN REFER-
ENCE BOOKS ON EARLY AMERICAN FURNITURE
CHOICE SAMPLES OF THE QUEEN ANNE, CHIPPEN-
DALE, HEPPLEWHITE AND SHERATON PERIODS
ALSO SOME FINE PIECES OF OLD ENGLISH FURNI-
TURE, STIEGEL & SANDWICH GLASS AND PEWTER

RARE HOOKED RUGS

WITH A FEW RARE PIECES FROM

MISS TRAVER'S PRIVATE COLLECTION

TO BE SOLD BY AUCTION
AT UNRESERVED PUBLIC SALE
FRIDAY, SATURDAY AFTERNOONS
APRIL SEVENTEENTH, EIGHTEENTH
AT TWO-THIRTY

THE ANDERSON GALLERIES
[MITCHELL KENNERLEY, President]
489 PARK AVENUE AT FIFTY-NINTH STREET
NEW YORK

CONDITIONS OF SALE

ORDER OF SALE

FRIDAY AFTERNOON, APRIL SEVENTEENTH

OLD PEWTER PLATES, CUPS, ETC.   1- 15

OLD STIEGEL AND SANDWICH GLASS WICK LAMPS, TUM-
BLERS, CREAMERS, SALTCELLARS AND OTHER
PIECES   16- 43

GROUP OF EARLY AMERICAN HOOKED RUGS, SOME WITH
FINE WORKMANSHIP AND DESIGN   44- 75

EARLY AMERICAN FURNITURE, ALSO A FEW OLD ENGLISH
PIECES   76-179

INCLUDING:
AN AMERICAN LATE 17TH CENTURY TWO-TIER PINE
STAND   102

MINIATURE MAHOGANY GRANDFATHER'S CLOCK, 2ND
HALF 18TH CENTURY   117

MINIATURE PINE GRANDFATHER'S CLOCK, AMERICAN,
ABOUT 1800   118

MAHOGANY "COFFIN" CLOCK BY AARON WILLARD,
ABOUT 1800   119

MAPLE SPANISH-FOOT BANNISTER-BACK ARMCHAIR,
AMERICAN, ABOUT 1700   137

CARVED CRESTED BANNISTER-BACK SPANISH-FOOT
CHAIR, AMERICAN, EARLY 18TH CENTURY   138

FINE CURLY MAPLE FALL-FRONT DESK WITH CLAW-
AND-BALL FEET, AMERICAN, LATE 18TH CENTURY   155

PINE SCROLLED CORNER CUPBOARD, AMERICAN,
EARLY 18TH CENTURY   159

RARE PAINTED PINE LOW CUPBOARD, AMERICAN,
EARLY 18TH CENTURY   164

SATURDAY AFTERNOON, APRIL EIGHTEENTH

OLD STIEGEL AND SANDWICH GLASS, INCLUDING SOME
VERY RARE PIECES FROM THE LAWTON COLLEC-
TION   180-198

GROUP OF RARE HOOKED RUGS, INCLUDING FOUR OF EX-
CEPTIONALLY FINE QUALITY, RANKING AMONG THE
FINEST KNOWN   199-230

GROUP OF FINE EARLY AMERICAN FURNITURE, CON-
TAINING IMPORTANT PIECES OF THE 17TH AND
EARLY 18TH CENTURIES, ALSO CHOICE SPECIMENS
OF THE CHIPPENDALE, HEPPLEWHITE, SHERATON
AND PHYFE PERIODS   231-339

INCLUDING:
MARTHA WASHINGTON SEWING TABLE BY DUNCAN
PHYFE   245

SMALL 17TH CENTURY BLOCK FRONT CHEST OF
DRAWERS   255

IMPORTANT DROP-LEAF "DIARY" TABLE, AMERICAN,
ABOUT 1680   262

RARE WALNUT TIP AND TURN TRIPOD TABLE, AMERI-
CAN, EARLY 18TH CENTURY   265

MAHOGANY THREE-PART DINING TABLE IN DUNCAN
PHYFE STYLE, AMERICAN, ABOUT 1800   272

SET OF EIGHT CHIPPENDALE MAHOGANY LADDER-BACK
CHAIRS, ABOUT 1760-70   280

IMPORTANT PINE WALL CUPBOARD, AMERICAN, ABOUT
1700   286

IMPORTANT CARVER CHAIR, MASSACHUSETTS, ABOUT
1650   291

IMPORTANT MAPLE SCRUTOIRE ON FRAME, AMERICAN,
ABOUT 1700   294

WALNUT VENEERED AND INLAID TRANSITIONAL HIGH-
BOY, AMERICAN, ABOUT 1700   298

UNIQUE CARVER CHAIR, AMERICAN, EARLY 17TH
CENTURY   299

HIGHLY IMPORTANT WALNUT GATE-LEG TABLE, AMERI-
CAN, 17TH CENTURY   307

CHIPPENDALE MAHOGANY BOOKCASE, ENGLISH, MID-
18TH CENTURY   311

IMPORTANT AND RARE CARVED CHEST ON STAND,
AMERICAN, 17TH CENTURY   315

IMPORTANT CHEST ON FRAME IN OAK AND PINE,
AMERICAN, 17TH CENTURY   318

RARE TURNED MAPLE JOINT STOOL, AMERICAN, ABOUT
1710   321

GROUP OF THREE EXTREMELY RARE WEATHER-
VANES, TWO FORMED AS COCKS, ONE AS INDIAN,
AMERICAN, 17TH, 18TH AND 19TH CENTURIES   322-324

AN UNUSUAL OFFERING

The rare and fine pieces to be dispersed in this sale present a splendid opportunity for collectors and other buyers to acquire specimens of Early American furniture that for character and quality are today seldom matched. The pieces come from the private collection of Miss Traver as well as from the general stock of The C. M. Traver Company.

The private collection is placed on sale because The C. M. Traver Company's lease expires within a year, and Miss Traver has determined to make a purchasing trip abroad this summer which will require all the storage space she has to house the resulting acquisitions. Many of these pieces have been illustrated and exhibited at various times, and have become well known to collectors of Early American furniture for their superlative rarity.

A conscientious effort has been made to describe accurately and attribute correctly each item. Very slight defects and unconcealed repairs have not been mentioned, the one being of no consequence, and the other quite apparent.

Miss Traver and The C. M. Traver Company guarantee every piece in this sale to be genuine as described.

CHARLES PACKER.

IMPORTANT MAPLE SCRUTOIRE ON FRAME
AMERICAN, ABOUT 1700
[NUMBER 294]

FIRST SESSION

NUMBERS 1-179

OLD PEWTER

NUMBERS 1-15

1 THREE OLD ENGLISH PEWTER MEASURES

ENGLISH, EARLY 19TH CENTURY

Two with shaped bodies, one cylindrical with flaring base, scrolled handles. (3)   *Height, 4 inches*

2 OLD PEWTER TANKARD   EARLY 19TH CENTURY

Cylindrical with moulded spreading base and scrolled handles, the flat cover mounted with a female head billet, and engraved with initials "G.H."   *Height, 9 inches*

3 OLD PEWTER WINE FUNNEL AND TWO PLATES

Wine funnel decorated with reeded bands. One plate with reeded edge, one with shaped edge engraved with crest. (3)

Diameter of funnel, 4⅜ inches; plates, 9 inches

4 TWO OLD ENGLISH PEWTER TRENCHERS

One with London mark, one with slightly damaged rim. (2)

Diameter, 15 inches

5 TWO OLD ENGLISH PEWTER TRENCHERS

With broad flanged edges. (2)   *Diameter, 15 inches*

6 TWO OLD ENGLISH PEWTER CHOCOLATE POTS

One cylindrical with reeded and beaded decoration, the other shaped and spirally fluted. (2)   *Height, 7½ inches and 8½ inches*

7 OLD ENGLISH PEWTER TODDY WARMER AND TODDY CUP

Interesting piece, oval with screw centre stopper and compartment containing "nightcap" cup.   *Width, 11½ inches*

8 TWO SMALL PEWTER BOWLS   CIRCA 1800

One with wide rim, the other with narrow edge. (2)

Diameter, 6 and 8 inches

9 OLD PEWTER PORRINGER AND PLATE
Porringer with pierced and scrolled handle, American. Plate with
reeded edge, engraved with crest. (2)
Diameter of porringer, 5⅜ inches; plate, 9 inches

10 OLD PEWTER LAMP AND MUSTARD POT
Wick lamp with circular bowl and tray base. Mug-shape mustard
pot with blue glass lining. (2)

11 EARLY AMERICAN PEWTER TEA CADDY
Unique heavy casket-shape tea caddy with domed top and shaped
base. Form, reminiscent of the Queen Anne period.
Height, 4⅞ inches

12 FIVE OLD ENGLISH PEWTER PLATES
Plain, circular with flat rims. Some stamped with makers' marks
and initials. (5)   *Diameter, 9 inches*

13 FIVE OLD ENGLISH PEWTER PLATES
Similar to the preceding. (5)

14 FIVE OLD ENGLISH PEWTER PLATES
Similar to the preceding. (5)

15 PAINTED TOLE TEA SET   ENGLISH, ABOUT 1810
Comprising a teapot, coffee pot, creamer, sugar basin and oval tray.
Painted with small landscape and figures, the remainder yellow and
black.   *Width of tray, 16 inches*

OLD STIEGEL AND SANDWICH GLASS, WICK LAMPS, TUMBLERS

CREAMERS, SALTCELLARS AND OTHER PIECES

NUMBERS 16-43

16 SANDWICH OPALESCENT GLASS FLOWER HOLDER
AMERICAN, 19TH CENTURY
Panel body, moulded edge, circular base.   *Height, 5¾ inches*

17 TWO EARLY AMERICAN GLASS WHISKEY BOTTLES
One, "Union" bottle with thirteen stars. The other, "Hunter &
Fisherman" bottle. Aquamarine color. (2)   *Height, 9 inches*

2

FOUR SANDWICH GLASS GOBLETS   AMERICAN, 19TH CENTURY
Rose-leaf design. (4)   *Height, 6 inches*

TWO EARLY AMERICAN BLOWN GREEN GLASS BOTTLES
Flattened bulbous shape, with hollowed scarred bases. Tapered and
collared necks. Dark and light olive-green color. Quart size. (2)

EARLY SANDWICH GLASS COVERED SUGAR BOWL
                                    AMERICAN, 1825-7
Heavy thumb-mould pattern.   *Height, 8½ inches*

TWO OLD SANDWICH GLASS WICK LAMPS
With graceful pear-shape bowls. One with cascade octagonal base,
the other with shaped stepped base. (Slightly chipped)   (2)
                                    Height, 10 inches

OPAQUE SANDWICH GLASS TABLE SET
                                    AMERICAN, 19TH CENTURY
Covered sugar bowl, creamer and spoon holder, with raised black-
berry design. (3)

PAIR OF OLD SANDWICH GLASS WICK LAMPS
Handsome specimens with tapered pear-shape bowls and scrolled
triangular bases, resting on lion's paw feet. An early type. (2)
                                    Height, 11¾ inches

PAIR OF EARLY GLASS RUMMERS
So-called "Thumping" glasses. Flaring bowls with heavy cylindrical
bases with tear drop. (2)   *Height, 4 inches*

SANDWICH GLASS OBLONG DISH
Canted corners, moulded edge. Snakeskin ground with crossed palm
and leaf design.   *Size, 8¼ x 6¼ inches*

PAIR OF LATE SANDWICH GLASS CANDLESTICKS
Fitted with electrical socket, light and cord and hand painted eight
inch "Ship" shades. (2)

**PAIR OF OLD SANDWICH GLASS WICK LAMPS WITH PEWTER
TOPS**
Gracefully shaped pair with inverted pear-shape bowls and stepped
quatrefoil bases. (2)   *Height, 11 inches*

28 **SANDWICH GLASS OBLONG DISH**
Canted corners, moulded edge. Snakeskin ground with crossed palm and leaf design.   *Size, 6 x 3¾ inches*

29 **SMALL WISTARBERG GLASS CREAMER**
Diamond quilt design, crimped handle. Slight rim chip. (*From the Temple Collection*)   *Height, 3¾ inches*

30 **PAIR OF OLD SANDWICH PRESSED BLUE GLASS SALT-CELLARS**
Oval basket-shape pressed in high relief with pineapple pattern. (Slightly chipped)   (2)

31 **PAIR OF OLD SANDWICH OPALESCENT GLASS SALTCELLARS**
Barge-shape, with scroll ends and feet, showing baskets of flowers on stippled ground. See Williams, S15, page 58. (Slightly chipped) (2)

32 **SMALL THREE-SECTION MOULD DISH**   STODDARD, N. H.
Quilted and paneled design, welted edge.   *Diameter, 4⅞ inches*

33 **STIEGEL TODDY GLASS**   AMERICAN, 1768-74
Plain body with heavy base. (*From the Lawton Collection*)
                                                      Height, 3¾ inches

34 **STIEGEL GLASS MUG WITH HANDLE**   AMERICAN, 1768-74
Leaf engraved bulbous body.   *Height, 5½ inches*

35 **SANDWICH GLASS BOWL**
Moulded edge, snakeskin ground with rayed and quilted pattern.
                                                      Diameter, 6½ inches
[SEE ILLUSTRATION]

36 **STIEGEL GLASS MUSTARD POT AND COVER**
                                                  AMERICAN, 1768-74
Diamond pattern. (*From the Lawton Collection*)   *Height, 4 inches*
[SEE ILLUSTRATION]

37 **STIEGEL GLASS MUSTARD POT AND COVER**
                                                  AMERICAN, 1768-74
Panel design. (*From the Lawton Collection*)   *Height, 5 inches*
[SEE ILLUSTRATION]

4

[35]   [42]   [43]

FINE EARLY AMERICAN GLASS
STIEGEL, STODDARD, N. H., AND SANDWICH

38 **STIEGEL FLIP GLASS**   AMERICAN, 1768-74
    Panel sides and engraved border. Very slight rim chip and self
    crack. Rings true.   *Height, 5½ inches; diameter, 4¼ inches*

[SEE ILLUSTRATION]

39 **PAIR OF THREE-SECTION MOULD TUMBLERS** STODDARD, N. H.
    Quilted and paneled. Fine quality.
                          Height, 4 inches; diameter, 3¾ inches

[SEE ILLUSTRATION]

40 **PAIR OF THREE-SECTION MOULD RUM GLASSES**
                                        STODDARD, N. H.
    Ribbed and paneled design.   *Height, 3 inches*

[SEE ILLUSTRATION]

5

41 MINIATURE THREE-SECTION MOULD CREAMER

STODDARD, N. H.

Quilted and ribbed design.   *Height, 3 inches*

[SEE ILLUSTRATION]

42 LARGE SANDWICH GLASS OBLONG DISH

AMERICAN, 19TH CENTURY

Canted corners, moulded edge. Snakeskin ground with thistle and crossed palm design.   *Length, 9 inches; width, 6¾ inches*

[SEE ILLUSTRATION]

43 SANDWICH GLASS TRAY

Brilliant snakeskin ground with acanthus leaf decoration.

Size, 6½ x 5 inches

[SEE ILLUSTRATION]

GROUP OF EARLY AMERICAN HOOKED RUGS, SOME WITH FINE

WORKMANSHIP AND DESIGN

NUMBERS 44-75

44 SMALL HOOKED RUG

Showing a spray of poppies in colors in a shaped green cartouche on tan ground. Bound. (Repaired)   *Size, 41 x 21½ inches*

45 HOOKED RUG

A design of tan scrolled leaves framing a raised floral medallion in indigo, ivory and crimson. Dark blue border.

Size, 5 feet x 2 feet 6 inches

46 HOOKED RUG

The field showing an octagonal panel containing well executed flowers in colors upon a dark green ground. Bound. (Repaired)

Size, 45 x 29 inches

47 HOOKED RUG

A mixed color field showing a retriever dog in the centre holding some unnaturally colored animal in its mouth. Bound.

Size, 38 x 25 inches

6

48 HOOKED RUG

Worked with a pleasing design showing a square centre panel with detached blossoms flanked at either side by large scroll leaves in vivid colors against a white ground, bordered in black. Bound.

Size, 3 feet 7 inches x 3 feet

49 SMALL EARLY HOOKED RUG

The field showing a scalloped diamond-shape cartouche with flowers in the centre, and double leaf motif at the corners. In soft colors upon a dark ground. Petaled cloth border. *Size, 38 x 27 inches*

50 HOOKED RUG

The tan field scattered with flowers and leaves in pleasing colors, framed by large scrolls. Apple-green border.

Size, 5 feet 10 inches x 34½ inches

51 HOOKED RUG

A posy of roses in rich colors upon a dark field framed by a key pattern border in ivory, indigo and rose.

Size, 3 feet 7 inches x 30½ inches

52 HOOKED RUG

Heavily worked with a geometrical and conventional floral design in rich mixed colors. Braided border. *Size, 50 x 31½ inches*

53 ANTIQUE HOOKED RUG

Worked with an oval panel containing a rose spray in deep colors upon a grey ground, framed with leaves in yellow and rose upon black. (As is) *Size, 4 feet 9 inches x 35 inches*

54 HOOKED RUG

Worked with a floral medallion framed by an oval leaf-entwined border on a dark blue-green ground. *Size, 42 x 27 inches*

55 HOOKED RUG

Showing a well executed design of raised flowers and leaves in pleasing colors upon a green and white ground. Lined.

Size, 54½ x 26 inches

56 HOOKED RUG

A basket of flowers framed by a rocaille cartouche, in soft colors on buff centre. Red arabesque scroll border. Bound. *Size, 48 x 28 inches*

57 HOOKED RUG

A central medallion of flowers framed by arabesque leaves with detached flower motifs at the corners. Pastel colors on grey. Braided border. *Size, 3 feet 6 inches x 2 feet 5 inches*

58 HOOKED RUG

With fine design of foliage and flower vines worked in pastel colors upon a black ground. Bound. *Size, 4 feet 11 inches x 2 feet 9 inches*

59 ANIMAL HOOKED RUG

The field showing a small bull framed in a shaped cartouche surrounded by semi-circular motifs and flower sprays, in colors upon a dark ground. *Size, 4 feet 5 inches x 2 feet 6 inches*

60 HOOKED RUG

The field showing an oval panel filled with flowers and leaves in bright colors. Floral border in soft pastel tints. (As is) *Size, 4 feet 6½ inches x 34 inches*

61 HOOKED RUG

Closely woven design in wool of two diamond-shape medallions containing sprays of roses. Soft colors. Bound. *Size, 4 feet 10 inches x 2 feet*

62 HOOKED RUG

Skillfully worked with naturalistic flower medallion framed by serrated leaves in rich colors on a light tan ground. *Size, 37½ x 27½ inches*

63 HOOKED RUG

Worked with a vari-colored sunburst centre on a field of olive-green. Arabesque scrolls in the corners. *Size, 4 feet 2 inches x 3 feet 9½ inches*

64 HOOKED RUG

Thickly worked. Showing a bright flowering tree in the centre, star motifs at the corners, remainder of the field covered with variegated colors. *Size, 57 x 37 inches*

65 HOOKED RUG

Closely woven. The field of ivory showing a diamond-shape geometrical medallion in bright colors, rose blossoms at the corners. Rainbow striped border. *Size, 3 feet 10½ inches x 28½ inches*

66 EARLY HOOKED RUG

Showing a floral medallion framed by large serrated leaves, in soft colors on a dark ground. Grey border with braided edge.

Size, 52 x 37 *inches*

67 HOOKED RUG

The field showing a raised wreath and two sprays of roses in striking colors upon an ivory ground. Black border touched with ivory and crimson. Bound. (As is)   *Size,* 5 *feet* 8 *inches* x 2 *feet* 6 *inches*

68 ANIMAL HOOKED RUG

The circular centre panel worked with a head of a pointer dog holding a pheasant in his mouth, remainder of the field worked with arabesque scrolls in rich colors. Charming specimen.

Size, 4 *feet* 3 *inches* x 2 *feet* 7 *inches*

69 HOOKED ANIMAL RUG

The buff-colored field worked with a black silhouette of a horse, framed by a border of semi-circular motifs. Braided edge.

Size, 4 *feet* 3 *inches* x 2 *feet* 9 *inches*

70 HOOKED RUG

Floral design of flowered dahlias with leafy stems, worked in striking colors upon a dark blue ground.   *Size,* 42 x 36 *inches*

71 HOOKED RUG

Worked with a geometrical pattern in alternating reds, yellow and blues, bordered by flowers and star motifs. Bound.

Size, 56 x 34 *inches*

72 HOOKED RUG

Almost all wool, showing a floral cartouche in soft colors framed in mauve upon a white background. Unusual colorings. Lined.

Size, 42 x 27 *inches*

73 SMALL HOOKED "WELCOME" RUG

Showing a cat and kitten playing with a ball; above, the word "Welcome", bordered with a semi-circular chain. Flowers and leaf in upper corners. Hemp lined. (Repaired)   *Size,* 40 x 25 *inches*

74 HOOKED RUG

Heavy pile with a spray of flowers in pastel shades on a white ground. Single leaf in each corner. Blue border.   *Size,* 52 x 33 *inches*

9

75 **HOOKED ANIMAL RUG**

The field worked with an oval panel containing a cat sitting on a tiled pattern floor with two playing kittens. Flower sprays at the end, dark border. (Repaired) *Size, 53 x 32 inches*

EARLY AMERICAN FURNITURE

ALSO A FEW OLD ENGLISH PIECES

NUMBERS 76-179

76 **EARLY AMERICAN DOLL'S FOUR POST BED**

An early piece. Turnings evidently whittled out. Shaped head and foot splats. *Length, 14 inches*

77 **PAINTED PINE DOLL'S CRADLE**

NEW ENGLAND, EARLY 19TH CENTURY
Length, 17 inches

78 **CHILD'S HIGH BACK WINDSOR ARMCHAIR**

AMERICAN, 18TH CENTURY

Oval back with ten spindles and moulded top rail, bent and extending to form the arms. Saddle seat. Bamboo turned legs and stretchers.

79 **CHILD'S MAPLE HIGH CHAIR** AMERICAN, 18TH CENTURY

Plain turned back posts with turned finials and two-slat back. Ring and vase turned front posts connected by double vase and ring turned front rings. Plain turned arms. Rush seat restored.

80 **CHILD'S SLAT-BACK ARMCHAIR** AMERICAN, 18TH CENTURY

Back with two arched splats between round posts with turned finials. Rush seat.

81 **CHILD'S SLAT-BACK HIGH CHAIR**

AMERICAN, EARLY 18TH CENTURY

Splayed legs finely tapered. Two shaped slats, ball finials, turned front and back rungs. Rush seat restored.

82 **CHILD'S SLAT-BACK ARMCHAIR**

AMERICAN, EARLY 19TH CENTURY

An example of the simple furniture built for children's use at the opening of the last century.

DECORATED SMALL MIRROR, "COURTING" TYPE
EARLY 18TH CENTURY

Moulded rectangular frame with shaped top, inset with small panels of painted glass; the top piece shows a basket of flowers. Has original pine case. *Size, 16 x 10¾ inches*

QUEEN ANNE DECORATED LACQUER DRESSING GLASS
ENGLISH, EARLY 18TH CENTURY

The shaped frame is painted with flowers on a green lacquer ground. *Size, 23 x 18 inches*

PAINTED PINE CANDLESTAND
NEW ENGLAND, EARLY 18TH CENTURY

Circular top on chamfered support, which stands on heavy circular base with three short peg legs. An interesting piece, entirely original. *Height, 29 inches*

SHERATON MAHOGANY MIRROR   AMERICAN, ABOUT 1800
Architectural style frame with fluted cluster columns at the sides, moulded and fluted shaped top. Mounted with two mirror panels. *Height, 44 inches; width, 24 inches*

MAPLE CANDLESTAND   AMERICAN, 18TH CENTURY
The square top has a gracefully turned and tapered centre support with out-curved tripod legs terminating in snake-head feet. *Height, 27 inches*

SMALL MAHOGANY MIRROR   AMERICAN, EARLY 19TH CENTURY
Reeded and moulded frame, and an original decorated blown glass panel above the mirror panel. *Size, 21 x 10½ inches*

PAINTED CANDLESTAND   TRAVER MODEL
This curious little piece was reproduced from a unique original. The column has a curious entasis and a pie crust necking and rests upon three legs, the feet of which are in human form, one bare, one stockinged, one slippered. The top is crudely decorated in black and red, on a cream ground with a large black bird and floral sprays. Note the similarity of the decorations to those of the Pennsylvania Dutch pottery. A most amusing piece.   *Diameter of top, 15 inches*

PAINTED CANDLESTAND   TRAVER MODEL
Similar to the preceding.

11

91 SMALL QUEEN ANNE MIRROR, "COURTING" TYPE

EARLY 18TH CENTURY

Shaped and moulded frame of walnut veneer on pine. The top is inset with small glass panel, painted with a pastoral subject.

Size, 21 x 16 *inches*

92 SMALL MAPLE TEA TABLE IN QUEEN ANNE STYLE

Circular top supported on four tapered legs with pad feet.

Height, 22 *inches; diameter,* 21 *inches*

93 MAHOGANY MANTEL CLOCK   AMERICAN, ABOUT 1820

Made by Ephraim Downes, of Bristol, Connecticut. Mahogany case in typical Eli Terry style. Scroll top with brass eagle finial. A painted glass panel below the dial.

Height, 32 *inches; width,* 17 *inches*

94 MAPLE TIP-TOP CANDLESTAND   AMERICAN, ABOUT 1760

Circular tray top of curly maple on a gracefully turned column supported by tripod legs ending in snake-head feet.

Diameter of top, 20 *inches*

95 WINDSOR HIGH STOOL   AMERICAN, 18TH CENTURY

Heavy circular pine top on four well turned vase-shape splayed ash legs, connected by bulbous turned stretchers. A unique specimen.

Height, 24 *inches*

96 PINE PIPE BOX   AMERICAN, 18TH CENTURY

Interesting piece, the front pierced with heart-shape motifs and carved with a small rosette medallion. A drawer in the lower part.

97 PINE PIPE BOX   AMERICAN, 18TH CENTURY

The top and front of box shaped. Remnants of old green paint add to its charm. A small drawer in the lower part.

98 SMALL WALNUT MIRROR, "COURTING" TYPE

EARLY 18TH CENTURY

Frame of walnut veneer. The shaped top is inset with a small painted glass panel.

Size, 15 x 10 *inches*

99 SMALL ADAM MIRROR   ENGLISH, LATE 18TH CENTURY

The maple frame contains panels above and below the glass, decorated with gilt classical figures and other ornamentation in relief, on an apple-green ground.

Size, 33 x 14½ *inches*

12

100 SHERATON MAHOGANY AND MAPLE SEWING TABLE
AMERICAN, ABOUT 1800

The mahogany top inset at the sides with panels of bird's eye maple. Ring turned and tapered legs with cuffed feet. Fitted with drawer.

Size of top, 18 *inches square*

101 SMALL MAHOGANY WALL CABINET   DUTCH, 18TH CENTURY
With arched moulded top and splayed ends. Fitted with shelves with shaped fronts and enclosed by shaped glass doors. Two small drawers in the base. Ball feet restored.

Height, 30 *inches; width,* 35 *inches*

TWO-TIER PINE STAND
AMERICAN, LATE 17TH CENTURY
[NUMBER 102]

102 TWO-TIER PINE STAND   AMERICAN, LATE 17TH CENTURY
Interesting early type candlestand with circular top and undershelf, banded in ash. On chamfered square support with cross trestle base. In the original finish. (Slightly restored)

Height, 28 *inches; diameter,* 15½ *inches*

13

103 CHIPPENDALE CARVED MAHOGANY CHAIR

ENGLISH, MIDDLE 18TH CENTURY

Interesting specimen of unusual design. The back is slightly curved and has a vase-shape centre and partly fluted round rails. Heavy carved cabriole legs with claw and ball feet. (As is)

104 PINE ONE-DRAWER CHEST   NEW ENGLAND, ABOUT 1700

An interesting transition piece. Has lift-up top with broad thumbnail moulded edge, a long drawer in the lower part, the frame with a heavy single arch moulding. The end stiles are shaped to form the feet. Interior has a till at one end. An interesting feature is the unusual lock to the drawer. *Height, 25½ inches; width, 44 inches*

105 TURNED LEG AND STRETCHERED TAVERN TABLE

AMERICAN, ABOUT 1700

The legs are turned in the double vase and ring pattern and connected with heavy rectangular moulded stretchers. The apron has a moulded edge and is fitted with a drawer which has the original wood knob. Framed oblong top of poplar. Maple base. (Slight repairs)

106 QUEEN ANNE SMALL WALNUT MIRROR

AMERICAN, 1ST QUARTER 18TH CENTURY

Moulded walnut frame with scrolled top. Contains the original beveled glass. *Size, 19 x 11 inches*

107 CHARMING PINE AND MAPLE SMALL TAVERN TABLE

AMERICAN, 2ND QUARTER 18TH CENTURY

Rectangular pine top with framed ends, on baluster turned legs connected by turned stretchers. (Restored)

Size of top, 28 x 21½ inches

108 PINE FIRESIDE SEAT   AMERICAN, 18TH CENTURY

High back with wing sides and shaped arms. Shaped base and lift cover box seat. Original. *Height, 37 inches; width, 19½ inches*

109   MAPLE SCREW CANDLESTAND AMERICAN, EARLY 18TH CENTURY

The screw turned shaft is fitted with adjustable two-light candle holder and has a circular raised edge shelf below. Base with four turned and raked short legs. (Candle cups restored) **Rare.** Exhibited at Carnegie Institute, Pittsburgh, Pa., in 1922.

Height, 5 feet 2 inches

110   HOOP BACK WINDSOR SIDE CHAIR

AMERICAN, LATE 18TH CENTURY

Seven-spindle back. Saddle seat. Bamboo turned splay legs and stretchers.

111   HOOP BACK WINDSOR CHAIR   AMERICAN, EARLY 18TH CENTURY

Back with moulded rail and seven spindles. Saddle seat; vase and ring turned splayed legs.

112   PINE AND MAPLE TAVERN TABLE   AMERICAN, ABOUT 1700

Rectangular pine top supported on turned vase and ring maple legs, connected at the base with plain stretchers. Drawer restored.

Size of top, 23½ x 39 inches

113   MAPLE CANDLESTAND   AMERICAN, ABOUT 1700

Has a circular beaded edge top with three splayed turned and bent shaped feet set into a heavy turned circular base.

Height, 20 inches

114   MAPLE AND PINE CHEST OF DRAWERS WITH BALL FEET

AMERICAN, ABOUT 1700

Rare chest of five graduated long drawers with moulded edges. Pine top and sides. Ball feet. (Restored)

Height, 41 inches; width, 38½ inches

115   CURLY MAPLE CHEVAL GLASS IN SHERATON STYLE

The rectangular mirror swings between a turned frame which stands on grooved trestle legs ending in chased brass feet.

Height, 55 inches

116   MAPLE WAGON SEAT   AMERICAN, 18TH CENTURY

Heavily constructed specimen. The double back has four slightly curved slats. Original green paint and splint seat.

Length, 32½ inches

15

117 MINIATURE MAHOGANY GRANDFATHER'S CLOCK

AMERICAN, 2ND HALF 18TH CENTURY

The case veneered with crotch mahogany and inlaid. The hood has broken arch top with original brass ball and eagle finial. Rectangular base with shaped bracket feet. Original finish. *Height, 38 inches*

[SEE ILLUSTRATION]

118 MINIATURE PINE GRANDFATHER'S CLOCK

AMERICAN, ABOUT 1800

Rectangular case with moulded cornice top, applied moulding on lower door and high moulded base with shaped front and sides forming the feet. In the original condition. **Rare.** *Height, 29 inches*

[SEE ILLUSTRATION]

119 MAHOGANY "COFFIN" CLOCK BY AARON WILLARD

AMERICAN, ABOUT 1800

Plain rectangular case with round dial and oval pendulum peep, having a brass urn and eagle finial on reeded plinth flanked by pierced curved brackets. Has the original works engraved "A. Willard, Boston". A rare clock.

[SEE ILLUSTRATION]

16

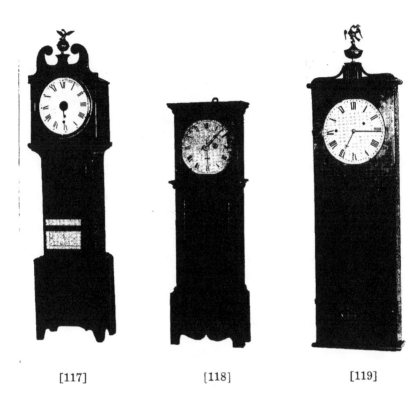

[117]   [118]   [119]

[NUMBER 117] MINIATURE MAHOGANY GRANDFATHER'S CLOCK,
AMERICAN, 2ND HALF 18TH CENTURY

[NUMBER 118] MINIATURE PINE GRANDFATHER'S CLOCK,
AMERICAN, ABOUT 1800

[NUMBER 119] MAHOGANY "COFFIN" CLOCK, BY AARON WILLARD,
AMERICAN, ABOUT 1800

120 MAPLE BANNISTER-BACK ROCKER

AMERICAN, EARLY 18TH CENTURY

High back with turned posts, shaped top rail and four split balusters. Rush seat. Turned legs and stretchers.

121 PINE AND MAPLE QUEEN ANNE TABLE

AMERICAN, 2ND QUARTER 18TH CENTURY .

Oval pine top, on four widely splayed maple legs which terminate in pad feet. *Size of top, 30 x 36 inches*

122 MAPLE CANDLESTAND AMERICAN, LAST QUARTER 18TH CENTURY

Plain circular top, on turned vase-shape and tapered support with outcurved snake-head legs. *Diameter of top, 17½ inches*

123 WINDSOR CHAIR WITH WRITING ARM AMERICAN, ABOUT 1800

The back has seven spindles and straight top decorated with stenciling. Fitted with broad writing arm. Commodious seat.

124 WALNUT AND GILT MIRROR IN QUEEN ANNE STYLE

Shaped upright frame ornamented with carved and gilt foliage scrolls and small vases. *Height, 53 inches; width, 19 inches*

125 BUTTON-FOOT THREE-LEGGED MAPLE TABLE

AMERICAN, ABOUT 1700

The fact that the turned mortise section of the legs of this table is about three inches in diameter points to an early date, as does likewise the simplicity of the entire design. This is seen in the straight beaded aprons and the dependence upon proportion for charm. The whole construction speaks of a period of primitive conditions in which furniture was sturdily built to withstand rough usage. Restored. *Diameter of top, 31 inches; height, 28 inches*

126 MAPLE QUEEN ANNE SIDE CHAIR

AMERICAN, EARLY 18TH CENTURY

The open back has a vase-shape centre splat, turned posts and curved top rail. Tapered front legs with pad feet, connected by a well turned stretcher.

127 FAN-BACK WINDSOR SIDE CHAIR

Yoke-top back with seven spindles. The legs and outside spindles of the back are in the graceful vase and ring pattern. Well shaped saddle seat. Bulbous turned stretcher.

18

128 **FAN-BACK WINDSOR SIDE CHAIR**
Nearly similar to the preceding.

129 **PINE AND MAPLE CANDLE STAND**
NEW ENGLAND, EARLY 18TH CENTURY
Oval pine top, on turned support with crossed trestle feet.
Height, 23 inches

130 **WINDSOR ROCKER** AMERICAN, MIDDLE 18TH CENTURY
Rounded back attached to spacing rail which extends to form the
arms. Wide oval seat. Widely splayed legs on original rockers. A
whimsical specimen.

131 **CHIPPENDALE MAHOGANY BUREAU**
ENGLISH, 3RD QUARTER 18TH CENTURY
A handsomely shaped chest of four graduated drawers with serpentine fronts. The chamfered stiles and borders of top and moulded
base showing fine leaf and fret carving. Bracket feet. (Slight re-
repairs) *Height, 34 inches; width, 36 inches*

132 **QUEEN ANNE SIDE CHAIR** CIRCA 1740
The spoon-shape back with vase-shape centre splat and carved top.
Slip seat, cabriole front legs connected by turned stretchers.

133 **HEPPLEWHITE SATINWOOD AND MAHOGANY OCCASIONAL
TABLE** ENGLISH, LAST QUARTER 18TH CENTURY
The rectangular top inlaid with various woods, the centre with a holly
leaf medallion. On tapered square legs connected by stretchers. A
drawer at one end, a blind drawer at the other.
Size of top, 23¾ x 17½ inches

134 **EARLY PINE CANDLESTAND** AMERICAN, MIDDLE 18TH CENTURY
Octagonal raised moulded edge top with slender chamfered pedestal
and bowed crossed trestle feet. *Height, 27½ inches*

135 **SHERATON GILT MIRROR** LATE 18TH CENTURY
Gilt architectural style frame with fluted columns at the sides sup-
porting a moulded pediment. The glass panel in two sections.
Height, 43½ inches; width, 22 inches

136 BALL-FOOT SCRUTOIRE   AMERICAN, ABOUT 170

The top has a fold-back and a let-down front panel showing a fitted interior of small drawers and pigeonholes. Four graduated long drawers in the lower body. Ball feet. Original iron drop handles and "H" and "L" hinges on flaps. Brass escutcheon of later date. In the original paint. A most unusual piece.

Height, 44 inches; width, 42 inches

137 MAPLE SPANISH-FOOT BANNISTER-BACK ARMCHAIR

AMERICAN, ABOUT 1700

Very fine specimen of this type. The well scrolled high back has four split baluster and finely turned posts with vase and acorn finials. Slender curved arms finishing with scrolls join the vase-turned front posts, which finish in Spanish feet and are connected by two well turned bulbous stretchers.

From the Private Collection of Miss Traver.

[SEE ILLUSTRATION]

138 CARVED CRESTED BANNISTER-BACK SPANISH-FOOT SIDE CHAIR   AMERICAN, 1ST QUARTER 18TH CENTURY

The high back has four split balusters and turned posts, capped by a handsomely carved and pierced scrolled cresting. Turned legs and handsome stretchers. Spanish feet. Old rush seat. Rare. Exhibited at Carnegie Institute, Pittsburgh, Pa., in 1922.

From the Private Collection of Miss Traver.

[SEE ILLUSTRATION]

20

[137]   [138]

[NUMBER 137] MAPLE SPANISH-FOOT BANNISTER-BACK ARMCHAIR,
AMERICAN, ABOUT 1700

[NUMBER 138] CARVED CRESTED BANISTER-BACK SPANISH-FOOT SIDE
CHAIR, AMERICAN, 1ST QUARTER 18TH CENTURY

139 **WILLIAM AND MARY HIGHBOY** AMERICAN, LATE 17TH CENTURY

Comprising a rectangular chest; in the upper part two small drawers flank a centre deep drawer, under these are three long drawers, the borders with herring-bone inlay in ebony and holly. Furnished with old engraved brass handles. This stands upon a base with three drawers in the large apron. Turned cup-shape and tapered legs connected by shaped stretchers. Ball feet. Cherry wood and sycamore side panels. (Base restored)

Height, 5 feet 10 inches; width, 3 feet 4 inches

140 **MAHOGANY DROP-LEAF CORNER TABLE**

ENGLISH, 2ND QUARTER 18TH CENTURY

Has square top which folds diagonally and forms a corner table. A pivoted drawer at one side. On round and tapered legs with pad feet. An interesting piece. *Width of top, 54 inches*

141 **PAIR OF FRUITWOOD SHERATON SIDE CHAIRS**

AMERICAN, LATE 18TH CENTURY

An interesting pair in rather unusual style. The shaped backs have four carved fern-shape splats. Upholstered seats. Tapered and fluted front legs with spade feet. (2)

142 **MAPLE QUEEN ANNE CIRCULAR DROP-LEAF TABLE**

The top consists of a centre leaf and two drop-leaves and is supported on four tapered legs with ring turned tops and pad feet. The apron is arched at either end. *Diameter of top, 48 inches*

143 **NEEDLEWORK AND WALNUT FIRESCREEN**

EARLY 18TH CENTURY

Mounted with a panel of petit and gros point needlework depicting a youth playing a lyre, surrounded by numerous animals, birds and trees. Carved frame of later date.

Height, 42 inches; width, 29 inches

144 **RARE HEPPLEWHITE RECLINING CHAIR**

AMERICAN, ABOUT 1785

This chair was obtained from one of the first families of Cambridge, Massachusetts. It had been secured by them some sixty years ago from the family of an old sea captain, who had it made to his special order of camphor wood which he obtained on a voyage to the East. The back is adjusted by means of notched brass quadrants. An under part can be drawn forward, making a foot rest, the legs of which fold under when not in use. The piece is in restrained Hepplewhite form. The back, seat and foot rest are caned.

22

145 PINE AND MAPLE SCRUTOIRE ON FRAME

NEW ENGLAND, 2ND QUARTER 18TH CENTURY

In two parts, the upper with a slant-front desk fitted with small drawers and pigeonholes, the flap supported with two pulls. Standing upon a maple base with shaped apron and Queen Anne legs with pad feet. Original iron staple hinges and small knobs. Original condition. *Height, 38½ inches; width, 34 inches*

146 UNUSUALLY SMALL BLOCK FRONT BUREAU

AMERICAN, ABOUT 1760

The blocking is of the positive type, with the concave section in the centre. The stiles have fine channel mouldings and top and base mouldings are well wrought. The piece rests upon straight bracket feet, through the shaped wings of which the blocking is continued. The large willow brasses are of fine contour and are genuine old ones. As some of them had been lost and replaced with knobs, it was necessary to complete the set. The piece retains its original patina.

Height, 31 inches; width, 3 feet

147 EARLY TURNED LEG MAPLE TEA TABLE

AMERICAN, ABOUT 1700

The circular top supported upon double vase-turned legs with pear-shape feet and braced by quadrangular stretchers. Broad splayed base. A genuine old piece. *Diameter of top, 30 inches*

148 SET OF TWELVE RUSH SEATED PAINTED SHERATON CHAIRS AMERICAN, EARLY 19TH CENTURY

The set consists of ten side and two armchairs. The backs are formed of three graduated slats between outflaring turned and chamfered back posts. The intermediate slat of the back is repeated as a foot rail between the front legs, but in a reversed position. The painted ground is of a warm yellow color and is paneled with brown lines. The head slat is naturalistically painted with a balanced cornucopia motif from which flow roses, foliage and fruits in effective colors. The arms of the two armchairs are probably a later addition.

149 HEPPLEWHITE MAHOGANY TRIPOD TEA TABLE

ENGLISH, LAST QUARTER 18TH CENTURY

Circular tray top on a reeded and water-leaf carved column supported by outcurving legs ending in snake-head feet.

Diameter of top, 21 inches

23

150 CURLY MAPLE SHERATON CARD TABLE

AMERICAN, ABOUT 1790

The curly maple top, and the form of the frieze, are of quatrefoil pattern, with square corners. The frieze is veneered with crotch mahogany and is centred by a satinwood panel. The reeded legs are slenderly turned. *Height, 29 inches; width, 35½ inches*

160

151 DOMED CORNER CUPBOARD IN PINE AMERICAN, ABOUT 1735

The opening is framed by a moulded arch based upon grouped pilasters which are delicately fluted. The pendentives of the arch display moulded and embossed panels and are crowned by a cyma moulded cornice. The semi-circular back is of matched boards, the dome is lath and plastered. The three shelves have finely shaped frontal margins. The base forms a low cupboard enclosed by two "H" hinged doors, with chamfered and arched panels. An unusually fine specimen. *Height, 7 feet 6 inches*
From the Private Collection of Miss Traver.

500

152 GRANDFATHER CLOCK IN FRUITWOOD AMERICAN, ABOUT 1800

The moulded case is inset with panels of curly maple. Architectural shaped hood with three vase-shape finials. The painted dial showing phases of the moon, etc. *Height, 8 feet*

250

153 SHERATON GILT MANTEL MIRROR

ENGLISH, LATE 18TH CENTURY

Architectural style gilt frame with acanthus bound fluted columns at the sides which support a moulded and trellised pediment decorated with lions' masks and drapery festoons. Canvas panel above the glass painted with classic subjects in the manner of Cipriani. (Slight defects) *Height, 6 feet; width, 5 feet 2 inches*

225

154 SMALL WALNUT AND MAPLE GATE-LEG TABLE

AMERICAN, 1ST QUARTER 18TH CENTURY

The nearly round maple top with drop leaves supported on walnut turned legs of the baluster and ring pattern connected by turned stretchers. Two pivoted turned gates support the leaves. In the original condition. *Size of top, 36 x 38 inches; height, 28 inches*

250

FINE CURLY MAPLE FALL-FRONT DESK WITH CLAW
AND BALL FEET, AMERICAN, LATE 18TH CENTURY

[NUMBER 155]

**155 FINE CURLY MAPLE FALL-FRONT DESK WITH CLAW AND
BALL FEET**   AMERICAN, LATE 18TH CENTURY

The slant top encloses a finely fitted interior of small drawers and
arched pigeonholes. The centre drawer is carved with a sunburst
motif and flanked by narrow vertical drawers with column pilaster
fronts. Has also a secret drawer. In the body are four graduated
long drawers. A carved shell appears in the centre of the moulded
base. Finely shaped brackets and claw and ball feet. Slight restora-
tion. A handsome piece.   *Height, 44 inches; width, 39 inches*

[SEE ILLUSTRATION]

156 CIRCULAR MAHOGANY LIBRARY TABLE ENGLISH, ABOUT 1820

The circular top with four drawers in the frieze is carried on a central
vase-turned column supported by three moulded splayed legs ending
in brass castored cups. Original brasses.

Diameter of top, 3 feet 11 inches; height, 28½ inches

25

157 SHERATON UPHOLSTERED MAHOGANY SOFA

AMERICAN, LATE 18TH CENTURY

Straight padded back, seat and ends covered in glazed chintz. Rounded arms inlaid with narrow panels of satinwood and supported by turned balusters. Four turned and reeded front legs. Curved square legs at the back.

Length, 6 feet

158 WILLIAM AND MARY CURLY MAPLE HIGHBOY

AMERICAN, LATE 17TH CENTURY

Very decorative piece. The upper part, a rectangular chest of two small and three large drawers outlined by channel mouldings. Standing upon a base with three drawers in the front and finely arched skirting, on six handsomely turned legs with bell shaped tops and ball feet, connected by shaped stretchers. (The lower part with some restorations)

Height, 5 feet 7 inches; width, 38 inches

159 PINE SCROLLED CORNER CUPBOARD

AMERICAN, EARLY 18TH CENTURY

A rare early specimen of generous proportions. The sides are splayed, and the whole body is outlined by a cyma curve moulding. Three curved front shelves graduating in depth. The sides and top of opening cut out in forceful curves. The lower body is enclosed by a moulded and chambered rectangular panel door with "H" hinges. The base is cut out to form supports to the piece. The old bluish-green paint adds to its attraction. An original with exception of feet.

Height, 6 feet 10 inches; width, 4 feet 2 inches

[SEE ILLUSTRATION]

160 QUEEN ANNE MAHOGANY DISH-TOP TABLE

ENGLISH, ABOUT 1730

This piece is noted for its slender and delicate proportions. The slim lines of the Dutch-footed cabriole legs are particularly good. This delicacy of the vertical members is further emphasized by the fine horizontal lines of the apron and top moulding. A genuine old piece in every respect except that the brasses of the drawer are not original.

Size of top, 32 x 20 inches

161 GEORGIAN MAHOGANY SIDE TABLE

ENGLISH, 2ND HALF 18TH CENTURY

Serpentined top fitted with three drawers. On tapered square legs with block feet. The piece has its original patina and its well proportioned form has real dignity and charm.

Height, 36 inches; width, 48 inches

162 SHERATON MAHOGANY SECRETARY

AMERICAN, LATE 18TH CENTURY

The upper part is fitted as a cabinet of small drawers, pigeonholes and compartments enclosed by a pair of paneled doors inlaid with holly lines. The lower part has a fold-over writing flap at the top and three drawers in the body. On short turned and tapered legs.

Height, 52 inches; width, 41 inches

163 MAPLE STOOL

AMERICAN, 18TH CENTURY

Square top and square splayed legs with square low and high stretchers. In the original red paint.

Height, 19 inches; width of top, 12 inches

27

164 RARE PAINTED PINE LOW CUPBOARD

AMERICAN, EARLY 18TH CENTURY

This extremely interesting and unusual shaped cupboard is in absolute original condition. The body is enclosed by a pair of arched and chamfered panel doors. The top is hooded and faced with smaller chamfered panels. On either side of this is a lift-up door on a slant, with unusual butterfly hinges revealing a space probably used to tuck away bonnets. A broad base moulding is carried around the front and ends. The feet are a continuation of the upright stiles.

Height, 50 inches; width, 40 inches

From the Private Collection of Miss Traver.

[SEE ILLUSTRATION]

28

165 FRAMED SILK NEEDLEWORK MAP OF THE BRITISH ISLES

ENGLISH, DATED 1806

Executed in silk chain-stitch on satin. Signed "S. Wilson" and dated. Black and gold glass mounting and gilt frame. *Size, 22 x 18 inches*

166 INLAID MAHOGANY BIRD CAGE

ENGLISH, EARLY 19TH CENTURY

Square, with rounded top; the front inlaid with a small medallion of Britannia. *Height, 14½ inches*

167 TWO SMALL INLAID MAHOGANY TEA CADDIES

AMERICAN, ABOUT 1800

One square with inlaid edges, the other casket-shape with sliding cover. (2) *Height, 4½ inches*

168 TWO OLD COLONIAL BETTY LAMPS

One in shaped box form suspended on wire. The other heart-shape, suspended on fish-hook spike. Both with linked chain wick pins. (2)

169 TWO EARLY AMERICAN IRON CANDLESTICKS

Suitable for electrical fittings in an early room. (2)

170 TWO EARLY AMERICAN WOODEN PLATES

Interesting early specimens of Pilgrim tableware. Rare. (2) *Diameter, 7 and 8½ inches*

171 INLAID MAHOGANY WORKBOX

AMERICAN, ABOUT 1800

Rectangular, the lid and front inlaid with a shell medallion in tinted holly. Borders are tulipwood. Brass bail handles at the sides. *Size, 11 x 8 inches*

172 **MAHOGANY TRAY** AMERICAN, ABOUT 1750
With well moulded saucer edge. *Diameter,* 14 *inches*

173 **OLD STAFFORDSHIRE FIGURE**
Standing kilted figure wearing a fancy coat and plaid hose, a dead
lion at his right. Entitled "The Lion Slayer". *Height,* 16 *inches*

174 **OLD STAFFORDSHIRE GROUP**
Two Scotch lovers seated in an arbor. Cream glaze with gilt.
Height, 14½ *inches*

175 **PAIR OF STAFFORDSHIRE FIGURES**
Lady with fruit, in delicate polychrome glaze. *Height,* 7½ *inches*

176 **OLD STAFFORDSHIRE PITCHER**
The shaped body modeled with a satyr's mask. With polychrome
and lustre decoration. (Spout chipped) *Height,* 6 *inches*

177 **POLYCHROMED STAFFORDSHIRE BUST OF SHAKESPEARE**
(Repairs) *Height,* 9 *inches*

178 **STAFFORDSHIRE NEPTUNE PITCHER** ENGLISH, 19TH CENTURY
Colored polychromed glaze. *Height,* 8 *inches*

179 **WEDGEWOOD BASALT WARE COVERED SUGAR BOWL AND
CREAMER**
Incised ribbed decoration. Base chipped on ewer. (2)

SECOND SESSION

NUMBERS 180-339

OLD STIEGEL AND SANDWICH GLASS, INCLUDING SOME VERY

FINE PIECES FROM THE LAWTON COLLECTION

NUMBERS 180-198

180 **EARLY SANDWICH GLASS COVERED SUGAR BOWL**

AMERICAN, 1825-27

Paneled thumb-mould pattern. *Height, 9½ inches*

181 **OLD SANDWICH GLASS COVERED SUGAR BOWL**

Octagonal with Gothic pattern decoration and stipple ground.

Height, 5½ inches; diameter, 5 inches

182 **OLD SANDWICH GLASS WICK LAMP**

Inverted pear-shape bowl on hollow bulbous stand and ribbed square base. Brass top. *Height, 12 inches*

183 **NINE SANDWICH PRESSED GLASS GOBLETS**

The bowls pressed with a pattern of vine leaves on a stippled ground. Plain circular feet. (9) *Height, 6 inches*

184 **SIX SANDWICH GLASS CUP PLATES**

Two conventional opalescent. "Wheel of Fortune". "Henry Clay". "Bunker Hill", and "Fleur-de-lys Eagle". (6)

185 **LARGE OLIVE GREEN GLASS BOTTLE**

SOUTH JERSEY, EARLY 19TH CENTURY

Moulded and slightly flattened bulbous shape bottle with short tapered and collared neck and scarred hollow base.

Height, 19½ inches; width, 13½ inches

186 **PAIR OF OLD SANDWICH GLASS WICK LAMPS WITH PEWTER TOPS**

Inverted pear-shape bowls with stepped shape bases. Fitted with electrical socket, light and cord and painted eight inch Godey print shades. *Height, 8¾ inches*

31

187 PAIR OF OLD SANDWICH GLASS WICK LAMPS
With octagonal stippled bases, inverted pear-shape bowls and pewter
tops. One repaired. (2) *Height, 9¾ inches*

188 OLD SANDWICH SAPPHIRE BLUE GLASS LAMP
With octagonal tapered bowl and flaring hexagonal base. Fine deep
color. Brass top. Rare. Fitted with electrical socket, light and
cord and painted ten inch Godey print shade. *Height, 9 inches*

**189 FIFTEEN PIECE PART TABLE SET OF EARLY AMERICAN
GLASS**
Comprising two covered compote dishes, two others without feet,
five goblets, covered sugar bowl, creamer, waste bowl, spoon holder
and two small salts. Snakeskin ground with quilted conventional
design. (15)

190 SAPPHIRE BLUE "PITTSBURG" GLASS BOAT SALT
Has name "Pittsburg" on stern. (Slight chip) *Size, 3½ x 2 inches*

191 SMALL STIEGEL GLASS DISH AMERICAN, 1768-74
Pale green. Spiral ribbing and welted edge. *(From the Lawton
Collection)* *Diameter, 4⅝ inches*

192 STIEGEL SAPPHIRE BLUE GLASS SALTCELLAR
AMERICAN, 1768-74
Slightly fluted. Hunter, type, fig. 69. *(From the Lawton Collection)*
Height, 2¾ inches
[SEE ILLUSTRATION]

193 WISTARBERG AMBER GLASS MUG WITH GREEN HANDLE
A rare combination of colors. *(From the Hunter and Lawton Col-
lections)* *Height, 4½ inches; diameter, 3¾ inches*
[SEE ILLUSTRATION]

194 BLUE STIEGEL SALTCELLAR AMERICAN, 1768-74
Plain surface, circular foot. *(From the Lawton Collection)*
[SEE ILLUSTRATION]

195 STIEGEL SAPPHIRE BLUE GLASS CREAMER
AMERICAN, 1768-74
Pear-shape body. Cylindrical neck. *(From the Lawton Collection)*
Height, 4½ inches
[SEE ILLUSTRATION]

32

[194] [193] |192]

[195] [196] [197]

FINE EARLY AMERICAN GLASS
STIEGEL AND WISTARBERG

196 EARLY AMERICAN GLASS JAR

Dark amber, with bulbous shape body. (*From the Lawton Collec-tion*) Height, 8½ inches

[SEE ILLUSTRATION]

197 STIEGEL SAPPHIRE BLUE GLASS CREAMER

AMERICAN, 1768-74

Indistinct paneling, slender bulbous body, circular foot. Extremely
rare type. (*From the Lawton Collection*) Height, 4½ inches

[SEE ILLUSTRATION]

198 EARLY PAIR OF EXTENSION PIPE TONGS AMERICAN

A most rare and curious example of iron pipe tongs.

33

GROUP OF RARE HOOKED RUGS

INCLUDING FOUR OF EXCEPTIONALLY FINE QUALITY

RANKING AMONG THE RAREST KNOWN

NUMBERS 199-230

199 HOOKED RUG
Closely worked with a design of squares containing zigzag and vertical stripes in rainbow colors. Bound. Nearly all wool rug.
Size, 58 x 36 inches

200 HOOKED RUG
The field in geometrical pattern well executed in rainbow colors. Bound.
Size, 52 x 34 inches

201 HOOKED ANIMAL RUG
Centre showing a retiring spaniel on a parquet pattern floor, framed by well executed vine border of flowers in bright colors.
Size, 4 feet 11½ inches x 31 inches

202 HOOKED RUG
Worked with posy of flowers in rich deep colors framed with flower vines, upon a dark background.
Size, 5 feet 3 inches x 2 feet 10 inches

203 LARGE EARLY AMERICAN HOOKED RUG
Beautifully worked with an all over geometrical design in pastel colors heightened with indigo. Bound.
Size, 7 feet 2 inches x 5 feet 5 inches

204 HOOKED RUG
An urn of flowers in bright colors against a dark ground surrounded by large arabesque scrolls. *Size, 4 feet 3 inches x 2 feet 11 inches*

205 HOOKED RUG
Heavy thick pile rug. The field of ivory white showing a central group of large blossoms framed by flower sprays, in bright contrasting colors. *Size, 5 feet x 2 feet 10 inches*

206 HOOKED RUG
Worked all over with geometrical squares in alternating colors of yellow, green, brown, and indigo. Bound.
Size, 4 feet 11½ inches x 3 feet 2 inches

207 HOOKED RUNNER

With flower and scrolls in rich colors on deep blue. Imbricated red and white border.　　　　　　　*Size, 6 feet 8 inches x 17 inches*

208 HOOKED RUG

Heavily and closely worked with a pot of flowers in bright colors in the centre of ivory field. Four borders in brown, turquoise, carmine and dark blue.　　　*Size, 4 feet 4½ inches x 2 feet 8 inches*

209 SMALL CIRCULAR HOOKED RUG

Worked with a conventionalized heart design in pastel colors upon a dark ground. Braided border. Part wool. *Diameter, 42 inches*

210 HOOKED RUNNER

With an all over snakeskin pattern forming a striking vari-colored design.　　　　　　　　　　*Size, 9 feet 4 inches x 22 inches*

211 HOOKED RUG

Charming floral design showing central cartouche of flowers upon a stippled grey ground framed by a wreath of flowers. Fine workmanship. Braided edge.　　　　　　　*Size, 75 x 37 inches*

212 LARGE HOOKED RUG

Worked with a striking geometrical design of stepped medallions in alternating light and dark colors giving a striking effect. Finely woven.　　　　　　　*Size, 6 feet 10 inches x 4 feet 5 inches*

213 HOOKED RUNNER

Showing a mixed colored field framed by three borders in shaded red, yellow and indigo.　　　*Size, 11 feet 10 inches x 26 inches*

214 LARGE HOOKED RUG

Early specimen. Beautifully hooked in all over design of squares containing rippled figuring in rainbow colors.

Size, 7 feet 2 inches x 4 feet 4 inches

35

215 HOOKED RUG

Closely woven rug with all over geometrical design of octagons containing quatrefoil motifs, in red, indigo and soft grey. Slight defects. *Size, 7 feet 4 inches x 4 feet 3 inches*

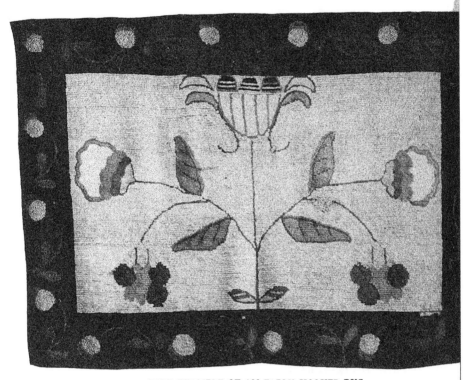

RARE EXAMPLE OF AN EARLY HOOKED RUG

[NUMBER 216]

216 RARE EXAMPLE OF AN EARLY HOOKED RUG

Hooked on a heavy homespun linen mesh. The centre with ivory colored ground showing a wide-spreading spray of archaic flowers and fruit, superimposed by a conventional American shield. The wide grey-black border quaintly worked in a repeat arched red and white fruit spray. All homespun materials were used in fashioning this rug. Illustrated in The Arts Magazine, February, 1925.

Size, 6 feet 5 inches x 4 feet 9 inches

From the Private Collection of Miss Traver.

[SEE ILLUSTRATION]

36

217 HOOKED RUNNER

Worked in braided style with design of quatrefoil motifs and small stripes in blue, yellow and red, yellow border touched with crimson. Bound. *Size,* 10 *feet* 8 *inches* x 20 *inches*

218 HOOKED RUG

Bright design of slightly raised flowers worked in beautiful colors upon a field of ivory white. Narrow chain border.
Size, 4 *feet* 9 *inches* x 2 *feet* 10 *inches*

ANOTHER UNIQUE EXAMPLE OF EARLY AMERICAN RUG CRAFTMANSHIP
[NUMBER 219]

219 ANOTHER UNIQUE EXAMPLE OF EARLY AMERICAN RUG CRAFTMANSHIP

This very early rug is fashioned by sewing layer upon layer of homespun cloth strips upon a homespun linen ground, shirring, fulling and scalloping to produce the desired design and effect. A centre panel shows an early house with a weeping willow tree on either side against a wavy sky background. The border has a meander design of leaves and concentric petaled flowers. Illustrated in The Arts Magazine, February, 1925.

Size, 4 *feet* 7 *inches* x 2 *feet* 3½ *inches*

From the Private Collection of Miss Traver.

[SEE ILLUSTRATION]

220 HOOKED RUG

Showing well executed design of flower scrolls in finely matched colors on pale green ground. An exceptionally good early rug hooked on old linen. Bound. *Size, 5 feet 3 inches* x *2 feet 5½ inches*

221 HOOKED RUG

The field showing a closely worked design of a large circular radiating star motif surrounded by flower vines, in bright colors upon a grey ground. *Size, 5 feet 6 inches* x *3 feet 4 inches*

222 EARLY OVAL HOOKED FLOWER RUG

Worked with a flower medallion frame by a wreath of flowers in bright colors on a dark ground. *Size, 4 feet 8 inches* x *3 feet*

223 HOOKED RUG

Showing a rich warm design of large flowers among leaves in shaded reds and greens touched with blue and yellow on a brown and tan ground. Bound and lined. A beautiful early rug.

Size, 6 feet x *3 feet 2 inches*

224 LARGE HOOKED RUG

With a striking design of serrated leaves in bright colors contained in an all over pattern formed by linked cartouches, shading from indigo to grey. *Size, 7 feet 2 inches* x *8 feet 8 inches*

225 HOOKED RUG

The buff-colored field showing a bold design of large rose blossoms and blue flowers with leafy stems, in rich colors. Border touched with black. Hemp lined. Bound. A beautiful early rug.

Size, 6 feet x *2 feet 9 inches*

226 HOOKED RUNNER

With tan centre field bordered with oak leaves in soft colors.

Size, 10 feet 4 inches x *23 inches*

227 HOOKED RUNNER

Unusually fine runner with attractive design of rose blossoms in shaped cartouches in bright colors on a tan and brown ground. Bound. *Size, 16 feet* x *2 feet 10 inches*

IMPORTANT EARLY AMERICAN NEEDLESTITCH RUG

[NUMBER 228]

228 IMPORTANT EARLY AMERICAN NEEDLESTITCH RUG

Worked on a background of homespun net in an over and under needlestitch. A small centre panel on black ground shows an early type house with flowering trees on either side. A whimsical meander border of tulip flowers and leaves frames the centre panel. With lovely texture and coloring. Illustrated in The Arts Magazine, February, 1925. *Length, 5 feet 4½ inches; width, 2 feet 8½ inches*

From the Private Collection of Miss Traver.

[SEE ILLUSTRATION]

229 UNUSUAL LARGE HOOKED FLOWER RUG

The field showing a well executed design of a central flower medallion in rich deep colors framed within a wreath of arabesque leaves in yellow and indigo. Similiar flower motifs at the corners. Tan and black ground. Slight defects.

Size, 8 feet 8 inches x 6 feet 2 inches

IMPORTANT EARLY NEEDLESTITCH RUG, AMERICAN, ABOUT 1820

[NUMBER 230]

230 **IMPORTANT EARLY REEDSTITCH RUG** AMERICAN, ABOUT 1820
This rug is fashioned upon a ground of homespun linen entirely in colored wools by a method known as reedstitch. It shows a silhouette of the packet ship " John Talpey " flying the Black Ball Line pennant, on an azure blue ground. On the left is presumably the fort at Governor's Island flying the American flag. At the right, a lighthouse also flying the American flag. In the upper centre and either corner, a five pointed star, and below on an olive-green ground, the name of the ship. Narrow mauve border with olive-green corners. A most lovely composition of color.
The Black Ball Line was established in 1816 as a line of packets between New York and Liverpool by some far sighted Quaker capitalists of this city, and sailed the first of every month. It was famous for the brutality of its officers and was probably the cause of the well known chanty—

> *In the Black Ball Line I served my time,*
> *Hurrah for the Black Ball Line!*

Illustrated in The Arts Magazine, February, 1925.

Size, 4 feet 11½ inches x 2 feet 7½ inches
From the Private Collection of Miss Traver.

[SEE ILLUSTRATIÒN]

GROUP OF FINE EARLY AMERICAN FURNITURE

CONTAINING IMPORTANT PIECES OF THE SEVENTEENTH AND

EARLY EIGHTEENTH CENTURIES, ALSO CHOICE SPECIMENS

OF THE CHIPPENDALE, HEPPLEWHITE, SHERATON AND

PHYFE PERIODS

NUMBERS 231-339

231 **MAPLE SLAT-BACK ARMCHAIR** AMERICAN, EARLY 18TH CENTURY
The back has two curved and two shaped slats, and round posts with gracefully shaped finials. The front posts have small mushroom-shape tops. Wave-turned arms. Splint seat (restored).

232 **SPINNER'S HICKORY AND MAPLE SLAT-BACK CHAIR**
AMERICAN, MIDDLE 18TH CENTURY
High rush seated chair with plain front legs and spindle bracing. Back posts with turned finials and three shaped splats.

233 **MAPLE TIP-TOP TRIPOD TABLE**
AMERICAN, LAST QUARTER 18TH CENTURY
Circular maple tilt-top on tapered and turned support with tripod snake-head legs. *Diameter of top, 39 inches*

234 **SHERATON MAHOGANY SHAVING GLASS**
AMERICAN, ABOUT 1800
Shaped rectangular stand is fitted with five small drawers, bordered with holly inlay. Two turned posts support the rectangular mirror.
Height, 29 inches; width 25 inches

235 **UNUSUALLY FINE COMB-BACK WINDSOR ARMCHAIR**
AMERICAN, MIDDLE 18TH CENTURY
Rare specimen with twelve bulbous turned spindles in the oval back and roundabout arms which end in well carved knuckles. Seven of the spindles run through to the top rail. Saddle seat. Vase-turned legs and bulbous turned stretchers. (Slight restorations)

236 **SHERATON MAHOGANY SEWING TABLE**
ENGLISH, LATE 18TH CENTURY
Charmingly finished small specimen with a pull-out drawer at one end and silk sewing bag beneath. A delicately turned cross-stretcher brace connects the square tapering legs. Delicate line inlay.
Size of top, 17½ x 13½ inches

41

237 MAPLE "DUTCH" CHAIR

AMERICAN, FIRST QUARTER 18TH CENTURY

Back with vase-shape centre, turned posts and curved top. Turned front legs and front stretcher. Fitted with rockers. Splint seat old.

238 ETCHED GLASS HALL LAMP WITH CHASED SHEFFIELD PLATE MOUNTS

EARLY 19TH CENTURY

Vase-shape etched glass shade with pierced and chased Sheffield mounts. Suspends from a bird with spread wings, with pulley fixture.

239 ADAM GILT MANTEL MIRROR AMERICAN, LATE 18TH CENTURY

The frame reeded and moulded in architectural style. Ball feet. Has the original glass panel in three sections framed by a leaf carved moulding. (As is) *Height, 16½ inches; width, 51 inches*

240 SLAT-BACK ARMCHAIR NEW ENGLAND, 18TH CENTURY

Maple and ash. The back has three arched slats between posts with turned finials. Shaped and undercut arms. Simply turned legs and stretchers. Splint seat.

241 SHERATON INLAID MAHOGANY SHAVING GLASS

AMERICAN, ABOUT 1800

Has rectangular mirror, swung between two turned posts. Bow-fronted base fitted with three small drawers. Holly line inlay.

Height, 23 inches; width, 23 inches

242 CHIPPENDALE CARVED MAHOGANY MIRROR

AMERICAN, 3RD QUARTER 18TH CENTURY

Rectangular moulded frame outlined at top and base with cut scroll-work. The top carved and gilt with a phoenix.

Height, 39 inches; width, 18 inches

243 COMB-BACK WINDSOR ARMCHAIR AMERICAN, 1775

An attractive example of popular type. The shaped comb-beam is supported on four spindles which rise from the spacing rail, the ends of which are prolonged, widened and shaped, to form the arms, which are supported on well designed vase turnings. The widely splayed legs show the same vase motif. Bulbous pattern stretchers. Pine oval saddle seat.

42

244 PINE AND MAPLE CIRCULAR TAVERN TABLE

CONNECTICUT, EARLY 18TH CENTURY

Has plain circular pine top on finely turned and slightly raked maple legs, connected by plain stretchers. Small section of top is restored, otherwise original. A very fine example.

Diameter of top, 28½ inches; height, 24½ inches

MARTHA WASHINGTON SEWING TABLE
BY DUNCAN PHYFE, AMERICAN, ABOUT 1800

[NUMBER 245]

245 MARTHA WASHINGTON SEWING TABLE BY DUNCAN PHYFE

AMERICAN, ABOUT 1800

If the statement that "the arched heading of inlaid panels is an infallible sign of Phyfe's work" be correct, then this piece is from his shop, as this form is used in the crotch mahogany panels of the inlaid blocks of the apron. The raising of the hinged top, with its arched ends, gives access to a small writing lid and fitments and to the covered compartments for sewing which occupy the two arched sections of the case. Below the frieze, which is veneered with well selected crotch mahogany, is a deep channeled section surrounding the entire table which is closely reeded, and at the front of this division is a door giving access to a drawer and two deep trays. The body is supported by a vase-turned pedestal with brass-capped flaring legs.

Size of top, 24½ x 13½ inches

[SEE ILLUSTRATION]

43

246 JACOBEAN HIGH STRETCHER TAVERN TABLE

AMERICAN, ABOUT 1700

90

The purpose of this peculiar construction has never been adequately demonstrated. The turnings are of the single reel type. The characteristically high side stretchers are mortised into a square block centering the legs. These tables are decidedly rare. Original throughout.

Size of top, 3 feet 8 inches x 26½ inches; height, 25 inches

247 MAPLE SPANISH-FOOT SIDE CHAIR   AMERICAN, ABOUT 1715

60

Straight vase-turned legs terminating in Spanish feet joined by bulbous stretchers. The cresting is better than usual as the depressed central section is boldly outlined by carved raying supported by the incoming whorl of the frame moulds. Rush seat restored.

248 MAPLE SPANISH-FOOT SIDE CHAIR

AMERICAN, 1ST QUARTER 18TH CENTURY

60

Moulded frame with slender vase-shape splat. Vase-turned front legs connected by boldly turned bulbous front stretcher. Side and back stretchers also turned. The frame painted black and touched with gilding. Original condition.

249 SHERATON CURLY MAPLE FOLDING CARD TABLE

AMERICAN, ABOUT 1800

260

Very decorative piece, with a shaped fold-over top and turned and reeded legs. Swell-front frame of mahogany, inset with oval satinwood panel.

Width of top, 33 inches

250 CHIPPENDALE CARVED MAHOGANY MIRROR

AMERICAN, MIDDLE 18TH CENTURY

80

Frame is handsomely cut with scrollwork and carved and gilt at the top with a phoenix. The glass panel is outlined by a narrow carved and gilded moulding.

Height, 39 inches; width, 23 inches

251 COMB-BACK WINDSOR ROCKER   AMERICAN, ABOUT 1800

60

Slightly conforming rectangular back with eight spindles, four of which continue up and are crested by a bow-shaped top rail. Straight arms with three spindles each. Raked legs with rockers.

44

252 CURLY MAPLE HIGH CHEST OF DRAWERS

AMERICAN, 18TH CENTURY

A chest of five long drawers; the top one deeper than the remainder;
the front of it moulded to simulate three small drawers and carved
in the centre panel with a sunburst motif. Moulded base with shaped
bracket feet.   *Height, 47 inches; width, 38 inches*

253 MAPLE BANNISTER-BACK SIDE CHAIR

AMERICAN, EARLY 18TH CENTURY

High back with turned posts and shaped top rail framing four split
balusters. Ring turned front legs connected by bulbous turned
stretcher. Splint seat.

254 BANNISTER-BACK ARM ROCKER   NEW HAMPSHIRE, ABOUT 1700

The outstanding feature of this chair is the bold yoke outline of the
headpiece with its curious circular and pointed ends. The turnings
are of the vase and column form common to the type. The arms are
of the moulded whorl-end Spanish type, and well formed. Rush seat.

[NUMBER 255]

255 SMALL BLOCK FRONT CHEST OF DRAWERS   17TH CENTURY

This interesting and charming piece was obtained from a descendant
of one of the early Dutch settlers in Northern New Jersey, some
thirty years ago. The entire body is veneered in a well marked wood
of a deep rich yellow, shading to brown. The square lines of the
blocking of the drawer fronts are carried through the skirt, which is
scalloped in the same curves. The top is cut out with curves, conforming to those on the drawers. The front ball feet are placed
under the outcurving pilasters, on the canted corners.

This piece is known to have been in this country for at least 225
years.

Height, 31 inches; width, 35 inches

From the Private Collection of Miss Traver.

[SEE ILLUSTRATION]

45

256 HEPPLEWHITE CARVED AND GILT MANTEL MIRROR

LAST QUARTER 18TH CENTURY

The oblong frame contains the glass in three sections. Surmounted by an urn of flowers flanked by foliage scrolls and festoons of flowers, which fall to the sides. Foliated paw feet. Original gilding.

Height, 47 inches; width, 56 inches

257 COMB-BACK WINDSOR ARMCHAIR   AMERICAN, ABOUT 1760

High back with bow-shaped top rail and seven long spindles running through the roundabout arms. Broad pine saddle seat. Vase turned maple legs. Bulbous turned stretcher. **Rare.**

258 HEPPLEWHITE MAHOGANY OCCASIONAL TABLE

AMERICAN, LAST QUARTER 18TH CENTURY

Charming little table on tapered square legs ending in spade feet. The top and apron are edged with ebony inlay. The drawer has an inlaid ivory key plate.

Size of top, 34 x 25 inches

259 MAPLE SLAT-BACK ARMCHAIR

AMERICAN, 1ST HALF 18TH CENTURY

The back has four arched slats between ringed turned posts with acorn finials. Simply turned front posts with small ball tops. Elongated sausage turned arms. Splint seat. **(Restored)**

260 APPLEWOOD AND MAPLE SLANT-TOP DESK

AMERICAN, 2ND QUARTER 18TH CENTURY

The slant top encloses a fitted interior of small drawers and pigeon holes and a central locker with secret drawers. Four graduated long drawers in the body, channel mouldings on rails and stiles. Moulded base with ogee bracket feet. (Slight restorations) On the bottom is written, "Fenton Z North bought this desk at Wm. P. White's sale the fall of 1863".

Height, 41 inches; width, 37 inches

261 HEPPLEWHITE MAHOGANY BOW-FRONT BUREAU

AMERICAN, LATE 18TH CENTURY

Its blond mahogany retains its original finish. A line inlay of holly is used to make a panel on each of the four drawers. The curves of the skirting and of the slender French feet are notably effective. Excellent original oval brasses. *Height, 36 inches; width, 41 inches*

IMPORTANT DROP-LEAF "DIARY" TABLE
AMERICAN, ABOUT 1680
[NUMBER 262]

262 IMPORTANT DROP-LEAF "DIARY" TABLE

AMERICAN, ABOUT 1680

This type of table is probably the rarest of all early American types. The oval top is of maple and its two drop-leaves are supported on drawbars. The legs are equally splayed in both directions, giving a broad floor base. Their turnings are an unusual stived combination of cupped-baluster, reel, and ring and cavea members. The stretchers are likewise unusual; they are placed with the broad surface parallel to the floor and their edges are finished with undercut cyma moulding. A section of top restored. A museum piece.

Width of top, 39 x 34 inches; height, 24½ inches
From the Private Collection of Miss Traver.

[SEE ILLUSTRATION]

47

263 SMALL WALNUT DROP-LEAF CORNER TABLE

ENGLISH, 2ND QUARTER 18TH CENTURY

Has a square top which folds diagonally, forming a corner table. On tapered round legs with pad feet. An unusual piece.

Size of top, 21½ inches square

264 SLAT-BACK ARM ROCKER

AMERICAN, LATE 17TH OR EARLY 18TH CENTURY

Back with four arched slats. Its early date is shown by the great reserve in the turnings and their close similarity to those of Carver type. The intermediate vase members of the front legs and the lined sausage turnings of the rungs, together with understructure of the vase-turned secondary brace beneath the arms, support this contention. The seat is restored, the rockers no doubt are a later addition.

265 RARE WALNUT TIP AND TURN TRIPOD TABLE

AMERICAN, EARLY 18TH CENTURY

This most unusual and interesting table has every feature of the William and Mary style in its design. The raised edge of the oval top is formed by a broad deep cove moulding. The turned centre support is of the same character as the legs of highboys of the period mentioned. The use of the double "C" scroll in the outspreading legs is absolutely unique. Illustrations of pieces of the period show it used in the vertical members only. Every detail indicates a seventeenth century piece, but it is probably of the early eighteenth century. The only example of its kind so far known. A collector's piece.

Width of top, 34 x 25½ inches; height, 27½ inches

[SEE ILLUSTRATION]

266 HICKORY AND MAPLE SLAT-BACK SIDE CHAIR

NEW JERSEY, 18TH CENTURY

Charming specimen. The high back has arched splats. Ring turnings and graceful vase-shape finials. Rush seat. Ring turned front legs and handsome front stretchers.

267 SMALL PINE AND POPLAR TAVERN TABLE

AMERICAN, 1690-1700

Charming Connecticut piece. The oblong framed top in pine. The unusually fine heavy turnings of the splayed legs in vase and reel form and the sturdy stretchers indicate an early period. Slight restorations.

Size of top, 30½ x 18 inches; height, 25 inches

48

RARE WALNUT TIP AND TURN TRIPOD
TABLE, AMERICAN, EARLY 18TH CENTURY
[NUMBER 265]

268 **MAPLE SLAT-BACK ARMCHAIR**   NEW ENGLAND, ABOUT 1700
High back has three graduated arched slats between ring turned
posts with baluster shape finials. Ring turned front legs and two
unusual ball turned front stretchers. Vase-shape supports to the
fine arms. Splint seat restored.

269 **PAIR OF SHERATON MAHOGANY SIDE CHAIRS**
AMERICAN, LATE 18TH CENTURY
The rectangular backs contain four slender delicately reeded columns
supporting carved pendentives with finely channeled and beaded
frames. The cresting rails are centred with enriched tablets. Tapered and fluted legs ending with spade feet. Seats upholstered.

270 **TWO SHERATON MAHOGANY SIDE CHAIRS**
AMERICAN, LATE 18TH CENTURY
One same as preceding, with haircloth covered seat. The other
slightly differing in the carving of the top. (2)

271 **CURLY MAPLE TURNED LEG AND STRETCHERED DESK**
AMERICAN, ABOUT 1700
The slant front encloses three tiers of small drawers and centre compartment. A long drawer in the body. On baluster turned legs connected by rail stretchers. Has the old brasses. Desks of this style
are rare.   *Height, 37½ inches; width, 35 inches*

49

MAHOGANY THREE-PART DINING TABLE IN DUNCAN PHYFE STYLE
ABOUT 1800-10

[NUMBER 272]

272 **MAHOGANY THREE - PART DINING TABLE IN DUNCAN PHYFE STYLE** CIRCA 1800-10

Handsome set of three tables with solid mahogany tops, each with a handsome columnar centre support which stands upon four reeded outcurved legs terminating with brass feet. The table is made to take two extra leaves and seats about sixteen people when fully extended. *Length,* 9 *feet* 10 *inches, extending to* 14 *feet; width,* 4 *feet*

[SEE ILLUSTRATION]

273 **SHERATON MAPLE HIGH POST BED**

AMERICAN, LATE 18TH CENTURY

Four handsome posts support the tester, the front pair finely fluted, and turned in vase shape, the bases square with block feet. Full size. The side rails were restored to lengthen the bed.

274 **QUEEN ANNE WALNUT MIRROR**

AMERICAN, 1ST QUARTER 18TH CENTURY

Rare early mirror in typical Queen Anne style. The upright frame is shaped at the top with cyma curves and has a scrolled and pierced cresting. Narrow moulded and gilt borders. Contains the original glass in two sections, the lower half beveled.

Height, 5 *feet* 2 *inches; width,* 2 *feet*

50

275 **HEPPLEWHITE INLAID MAHOGANY BUREAU**

NEW JERSEY, ABOUT 1790

Attractive large chest of four drawers. The deep top bonnet drawer has a wide central lentoid panel of crotch mahogany flanked by lozenge shaped panels with inlaid floral ovals. Shaped valance and French feet. Original oval brasses.

Height, 46 inches; width, 46 inches

276 **UNUSUAL HEPPLEWHITE MAHOGANY SEWING TABLE**

AMERICAN, ABOUT 1790

Octagonal top and apron banded with satinwood. On tapered and turned legs with graceful connecting cross stretcher. The top is hinged to give access to the sewing fitments and bag.

Height, 30 inches; width, 20½ inches

277 **CURLY MAPLE BALL-AND-CLAW FOOT DROP-LEAF TABLE**

AMERICAN, ABOUT 1740

The end aprons are well shaped, in a double cyma curve, and the bird's claw-and-ball feet well executed. The drop leaves are supported on pivoted legs.

Diameter of top, 38 inches

278 **SMALL WALNUT AND VENEERED INLAID CHEST OF DRAWERS**

AMERICAN, ABOUT 1695

The top is delicately moulded and veneered with matched burl-walnut with double cross grain borders of the same wood, between holly line. Two small and two large drawers are paneled in walnut and have cross grain borders set off with a narrow holly inset. The stiles have the early single-arch moulding. Above the Dutch ball feet is a cyma and filet base mould. American chests of this character are extremely rare, and that this one belongs to that category is determined by the fact that the entire interior is of pine and constructed in the American manner. The tear drop handles are not original.

Height, 31 inches; width, 32 inches

279 **CHERRY SCRUTOIRE ON FRAME**

NEW ENGLAND, 2ND QUARTER 18TH CENTURY

Slant top enclosing a row of small drawers with shaped pigeonholes above, the borders with narrow diaper and line inlay. Four long graduated drawers in the body furnished with old brasses. The stand with shaped skirting and short well designed cabriole legs and pad feet. A rare piece. In the original finish.

Height, 42 inches; width, 37 inches

EIGHT CHIPPENDALE MAHOGANY LADDER-BACK CHAIRS, 1760-70
[NUMBER 280]

280 **EIGHT CHIPPENDALE MAHOGANY LADDER-BACK CHAIRS**

ABOUT 1760-70

1400

Comprising a pair of well proportioned arm chairs and six side
chairs. The shaped backs in the ladder type have four curved and
pierced splats, carved in the centres with foliage and shell ornament.
The arm chairs have partly fluted and voluted arms. The carving
on the backs of the side chairs is slightly different in detail from that
of the arm chairs. Upholstered seats, moulded square legs connected
by plain stretchers with carved corner bracing at the tops. (Some
with slight restorations) **Of exceptional quality.**

[SEE ILLUSTRATION]

52

281 **MAHOGANY PIE CRUST TABLE** AMERICAN, ABOUT 1760
This table was discovered in Exeter, New Hampshire, and with the
exception of the drift pin attaching the column to the cage, is entirely original. Its unusual feature consists in the breeched, stockinged and slippered legs, of human form, which support the pedestal
block. The form of this block approximates a Queen Anne model and
would indicate an earlier date for the piece than that assigned. The
column is turned in an attractive baluster pattern and carries the
columned cage upon which the top spins and tips. A collector's
piece. *Diameter of top, 23½ inches; height, 29 inches*

282 **IMPORTANT INLAID BOW-FRONT BUREAU**
AMERICAN, ABOUT 1785
The body is of blond mahogany and the four beaded drawers are
edged with cross grain kingwood with a delicate inner guard of
checkered ebony, holly and tulipwood. The top edge bears a line
of ornamental inlay corresponding to that banding the piece above
the shaped skirt. The French feet and original brasses, of unusual
form, are added attractions. American bureaus of this rich quality
are now seldom seen. *Height, 37 inches; width, 42 inches*

283 **PAIR OF FLEMISH STYLE CANE CHAIRS**
AMERICAN, LATE 17TH CENTURY
Rare pair of the "Flemish" chairs so-called because of the scroll
carving which is of this origin. High backs with turned posts and
scrolled carved cresting framing cane panels. Turned legs connected by stretchers with front stretcher matching the top. Cane
seat. These chairs came from a New England Collection.

284 **PAIR OF FLEMISH STYLE CANE CHAIRS**
AMERICAN, LATE 18TH CENTURY
Same as preceding.

285 **LARGE QUEEN ANNE WALNUT FRAMED MIRROR**
ABOUT 1720-40
This unusually large mirror has a narrow moulded frame. The top
shaped in curves typical of the period. The two panels of glass with
beveled edges, the upper following the outline of the frame. A
desirable piece. *Height, 62 inches; width, 28 inches*

286 **IMPORTANT PINE WALL CUPBOARD**   AMERICAN, ABOUT 1700
In the upper part are two shaped shelves with curved fronts and
undercut edges outlined by a scrolled framework of cyma and cavea
cutting.   The top has a bold cornice.   The lower body is enclosed by
a single door with a broadly chamfered and moulded panel and has
the original butterfly hinges.   Forceful evidence of the age of the
piece are the deeply worn hand marks around the top framing of the
door.   Specimens of such quality as the present piece are extremely
rare. Entirely original. Exhibited at Carnegie Institute, Pittsburgh,
Pa., in 1922.   *Height, 6 feet 5 inches; width, 3 feet*
From the private Collection of Miss Traver.

[SEE ILLUSTRATION]

287 **SMALL PINE AND MAPLE OVAL TOP TABLE**
AMERICAN, ABOUT 1700
An unusual specimen, having very fine double vase and ring turned
maple legs and turned stretchers (unique feature).   Ogee moulded
aprons.   Oval pine top.   In the original condition.
Size of top, 31 x 23 inches; height, 24½ inches

288 **QUEEN ANNE MAHOGANY LOWBOY**
AMERICAN, 2ND QUARTER 18TH CENTURY
Charming piece with one long and three small drawers in the front.
The centre drawer carved with sunburst ornament, shaped skirting
around the lower part, with handsomely ornamented pendent finials.
Overlapping top with thumb-nail edge.   On restrained cabriole legs
with pad feet.   An original piece, including brasses.
Height, 30 inches; width, 35 inches

289 **CHIPPENDALE MAHOGANY CARD TABLE**
AMERICAN, MIDDLE 18TH CENTURY
Fold-over shaped top with deeply scored pockets for counters and
squared sunken corners for candlesticks.   Fitted with a drawer.   On
cabriole legs with claw and ball feet.   *Width of top, 33 inches*

290 **QUEEN ANNE WALNUT LIBRARY TABLE**
AMERICAN, ABOUT 1740
The legs are slightly splayed, tapered and turned variety, resting
on Dutch feet.   Below the top with its shaped cleats a deep central
drawer is flanked by two smaller ones.   An example of the sturdy
practical furniture of the mid-eighteenth century.
Size of top, 5 x 3 feet

54

IMPORTANT PINE WALL CUPBOARD
AMERICAN, ABOUT 1700

[NUMBER 286]

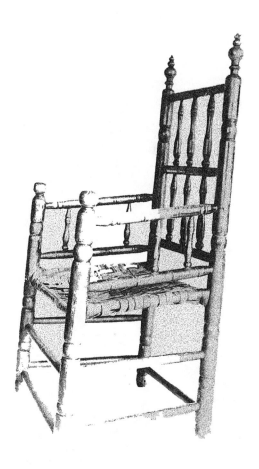

291 **IMPORTANT CARVER CHAIR**   MASSACHUSETTS, ABOUT 1650
In this example is seen the transitional type between the Carver and
the Brewster designs. The row of three upright spindles beneath
the arms is of the latter origin. The two rows of back spindles and
the arm spindles are turned in the vase-and-blunt-arrow pattern
of the Carver type. Back and front posts have bulb turnings spaced between the points of junction of the rail spindles. The
front posts have ball terminals, while the finials of the back posts
consist of three graduated ball turnings above a slim collared necking. The broken splint seat is original. (Slight restorations.) Illustrated in "Nutting", 1st Edition, page 188. (*From the Behrend
Collection*)
From the Private Collection of Miss Traver.

292 **CARVER ARMCHAIR** AMERICAN, MIDDLE 17TH CENTURY
The chiseled-ring posts all bear a single abruptly turned vase member which breaks the plain cylindrical turning. The front posts carry their original ball finials while the collared and spheroid members forming the finials of the back posts are likewise original. This is a rare feature, as the finials of most examples will be found to be restorations. Three blunt arrow and reel turned spindles between plainly turned containing rungs form the back, above which is a strongly turned cresting rail of paired double-vase turnings with ball and bead necking. The arms and rungs are cylindrical turnings with heavy bead ends. Splint seat restored and legs extended. A brilliant example of this rare type.

293 **CHILD'S SLAT-BACK ARMCHAIR** AMERICAN, ABOUT 1690
There is seen in this chair the use of turn forms associated with the Carver period. Note the crude double-vase turnings of the extensions of the front legs and the form of the turned arms. The tooled lines of the back posts also suggest an early date. Rush seat restored.

294 **IMPORTANT MAPLE SCRUTOIRE ON FRAME**

AMERICAN, ABOUT 1700
One of the finest examples of this style that have come to light. The slant top encloses small drawers and arched pigeonholes with a centre compartment that slides out by manipulating a secret spring disclosing secret drawers at the back. Underneath is a well with sliding cover. In the lower body is a shallow drawer below a simulated drawer front. A moulded finish at bottom. This stands on a turned leg and stretchered base of the vase and ring type. An unusual feature is the position of the long stretchers which are joined to the leg about midway from the floor. The skirt is cut in cyma curves similar to those on the six legged highboys. Minor restorations. In the original finish.

Height, 38 inches; width, 33½ inches
From the Private Collection of Miss Traver.

[SEE ILLUSTRATION FACING PAGE 1 OF TEXT]

295 **OX-BOW FRONT MAHOGANY BUREAU**   AMERICAN, ABOUT 1765
These small bureaus, with inverted serpentine fronts, are rare. The four drawers have richly figured crotched mahogany fronts. The top has splayed corners and ogee-moulded edges. The base mould is of virile type. Finely shaped ogee bracket feet. Old brasses. An attractive piece in the original finish.

Height, 31 *inches; width,* 37 *inches*

296 **CURLY MAPLE CIRCULAR DROP-LEAF TABLE WITH CLAW-AND-BALL FEET**   AMERICAN, MIDDLE 18TH CENTURY
Charming small table with drop-leaf top supported on four cabriole legs terminating in claw-and-ball feet. Apron shaped at either end. An unusually good example in maple.   *Diameter of top,* 38 *inches*

297 **CURLY MAPLE SLANT-TOP DESK**

AMERICAN, LATE 17TH CENTURY
Unusually rare and early piece. Slant top enclosing a finely fitted interior of arched pigeonholes and small drawers. The end drawers project forward about four inches. Two small and three long drawers in the body, the framing faced by channel moulding. The drawers are furnished with old engraved brass handles. Moulded base with the original ball feet. (Minor restorations only.)

Height, 41½ *inches; width,* 35 *inches*

298 **WALNUT VENEERED AND INLAID TRANSITIONAL HIGHBOY**
AMERICAN, ABOUT 1700
The drawers are faced in crotched walnut veneered and edged with herring-bone inlay. Around the drawers and frame are canal mouldings. The upper body has four long drawers above three short ones. The lower body, supported by cabriole legs with pad feet, is fitted with a long shallow drawer below which are two square drawers with a shallow one between. The outline of the beautifully shaped skirt is unusual in that it provides for three pendent ornaments. The engraved handles with bent wire fastenings are original with exception of three. (Minor restorations only.)

Height, 6 *feet; width,* 3 *feet* 3 *inches*
From the Private Collection of Miss Traver.

[SEE ILLUSTRATION]

58

WALNUT VENEERED AND INLAID TRANSITIONAL
HIGHBOY, AMERICAN, ABOUT 1700

[NUMBER 298]

299 UNIQUE CARVER CHAIR AMERICAN, EARLY 17TH CENTURY

Nutting, in his "Furniture of the Pilgrim Century", deplores the fact that the connecting links between the Carver chairs and earlier sixteenth century examples seem to be missing. This chair is one of those missing links, and shows closer affinity to the early Varangian Guard chairs than any known specimen of the American chairmaker's art. It is likewise a connecting link between the Carver and mushroom slat-back types. We see here the mushroom terminal of the front leg in combination with a back closely related to the Carver group, although consisting of a single section of spindles which are much longer, fitting the entire back, than those of the typical Carver chair. The reversed and collared double-vase forms of the back spindles and posts are strongly reminiscent of the Varangian chair, while the serpentined form of the turning, below the bold mushroom terminal of the front legs, is even more strongly so. This character is again impressed by the virility of the bead, filet and cavea turned arms, which are the largest in diameter at present known. The finials of the back posts and extensions of feet are restorations, otherwise the chair is in original condition. Exhibited at Carnegie Institute, Pittsburgh, Pa., in 1922. Constructed of American maple throughout.

From the Private Collection of Miss Traver.

[SEE ILLUSTRATION]

300 HEPPLEWHITE MAHOGANY ARTIST'S TABLE

ENGLISH, LATE 18TH CENTURY

A very unusual specimen. The rectangular top fitted with adjustable flap, a drawer and two candle slides edged with inlay. The centre support fluted and leaf carved. The outcurving legs terminating in snake-head feet. *Height, 32¼ inches*

301 EARLY OAK AND PINE CHEST WITH TWO DRAWERS

CONNECTICUT, LAST QUARTER 17TH CENTURY

An unusual specimen of Hadley form without any decoration. The ends are constructed with a single panel while the front, above the drawers, is formed with three panels contained within chamfered stiles. The turned feet are extensions of the single posts. The top is finished with thumb-nail moulding. In the lower part are two drawers. Very rare. *Height, 42 inches, width, 42 inches*

60

UNIQUE CARVER CHAIR
AMERICAN, EARLY 17TH CENTURY
[NUMBER 299]

302 WILLIAM AND MARY SCROLL TOP WALNUT MIRROR

LATE 17TH CENTURY

Characteristic of the period. The frame nearly square, with broad ovolo moulding in oyster-shell veneer surmounted by a scrolled and pierced cresting, the fret design of which is of birds and foliated scrolls. Unique in that it is entirely original, including the cresting.

Height, 34 inches; width, 23½ inches

303 CARVER ARMCHAIR

AMERICAN, 17TH CENTURY

The back and front posts display squat ball turnings between the structural points. The four spindles of the back have the closed ball-and-blunt-arrow turning typical of the period. The arms are sausage turned while the finials are of an unusual pattern. Originally this chair had a splint seat. The ball turnings which top the front posts are restorations. Similar to one shown by Nutting.

304 PINE DRESSER

CONNECTICUT, ABOUT 1720

A charming piece, constructed in mellow old pine and poplar. The upper part is fitted with three open shelves, grooved for plates. The framing is rectangular and faced by a moulding of unusual pattern, a part of which has been restored. The lower part is a cupboard containing one shelf and enclosed by a pair of chamfered panel doors having the original wood knob. Mouldings similar to those on the upper part frame the lower body. Cutout ends form the feet. "H" hinges.

Height, 6 feet 8 inches; width, 4 feet 3 inches

305 MAHOGANY DROP-LEAF BREAKFAST TABLE

AMERICAN, 2ND QUARTER 18TH CENTURY

Rectangular top with two deep drop-leaves, supported by two instead of one of the legs as is usually found, making a total of six restrained cabriole legs with pad feet. The apron at either end is finely shaped. A fine specimen.

Size of top, 51½ x 48 inches

306 PINE BALL-FOOT CHEST OF DRAWERS AMERICAN, ABOUT 1700

These pieces fitted with drawers only are rare. Has four long drawers; around them and on the frame is a wide single-arch moulding. The frame is finished at top and bottom with projecting mouldings. The four ball feet are original. Minor restorations. A very desirable piece.

Height, 37½ inches; width, 39¾ inches

From the Private Collection of Miss Traver.

HIGHLY IMPORTANT WALNUT GATE-LEG TABLE
AMERICAN, 17TH CENTURY
[NUMBER 307]

307 **HIGHLY IMPORTANT WALNUT GATE-LEG TABLE**

AMERICAN, 17TH CENTURY

It is generally believed that these handsome gate-leg tables, when
made of Virginia walnut, are of Southern origin. This specimen
is supposed to have been found in Connecticut. Nutting remarks
that "it is possible that the wood was brought there from the South
and locally worked". The size, the purity of the vase turnings, the
great width of bed, with its scalloped aprons and drawers, all con-
tribute to the dignity of this example. This table is a remarkable
specimen in absolute original condition. Exhibited at Carnegie Institute, Pittsburgh, Pa., in 1922.

Size of top, 63 x 54 *inches; height,* 26 *inches*

From the Private Collection of Miss Traver.

63

308 **SATINWOOD AND MAHOGANY SEWING TABLE**

AMERICAN, ABOUT 1790

Fitted with two drawers, one compartmented. Below the drawers is a sliding frame (restored) which bore a bag. The faces of the drawers and aprons are paneled in curly and branch satinwood. The apron edge is banded with that rare, shaded, concentrated spheroid pattern of inlay which is credited by some to Phyfe. The gracefully turned legs are reeded, the upper block halved and attached to the splayed corners. One drawer partly restored. A rare and highly desirable specimen. *Height, 31 inches; top, 20½ x 16 inches*

309 **MAPLE GATE-LEG TABLE** AMERICAN, ABOUT 1700

The top is rectangular and has two deep drop-leaves supported on pull-out gates. The legs have unusually good balanced vase and reel turning and are connected by turned stretchers. In original condition. Rare. *Size of top, 44 inches square*

From the Private Collection of Miss Traver.

310 **RARE WALNUT DAYBED** NEW ENGLAND, LATE 17TH CENTURY

The splayed back-rest has a crescent-centred, double-cyma scrolled cresting rail, and its legs are square, whereas the other six legs of the base, together with their stretchers, are turned in ring-centred double-vase pattern. The legs rest upon ball feet. A collector's piece of rarity. *Height, of head-rest, 35 inches; width, 24 inches*

311 **CHIPPENDALE MAHOGANY SECRETARY BOOKCASE**

ENGLISH, MIDDLE 18TH CENTURY

Finely constructed piece in solid mahogany. The upper part fitted with adjustable shelves and three drawers, enclosed by a pair of Gothic pattern glass doors, with handsome mouldings framing the mullions. Top with broken-arch cornice with dentelled and carved borders, also centre urn and flame finial. The lower part with slant top enclosing fine interior of small drawers and shaped pigeonholes with carved fronts. Four long drawers in the lower body. Base with carved ogee bracket feet. *Height, 8 feet; width, 3 feet 6 inches*

[SEE ILLUSTRATION]

64

CHIPPENDALE MAHOGANY SECRETARY BOOKCASE
ENGLISH, MID-18TH CENTURY

[NUMBER 311]

312 **JACOBEAN LIBRARY TABLE**   AMERICAN, ABOUT 1695

The underbody is constructed with oak legs and stretchers. The deep apron is bordered by a bold cyma moulding, below which its edge is shaped in minute repeated cyma scallops. The legs are formed from stock over two and a half inches square and, although of baluster pattern, are not turned, but rounded and shaped by hand. The apron is fitted with a deep drawer and the shaped top cleats are pegged outside the legs. The top is of American walnut. An unusually good example of its type. (Drawer restored)

Length, 54 x 32 *inches*

313 **EARLY PINE AND POPLAR BALL-FOOT DESK**

CONNECTICUT, ABOUT 1690

The slant top encloses a fitted interior of small drawers with wooden knobs, pigeonholes and well head with sliding cover. The lid with original broad iron hinges. Double-arch moulding on the stiles divides the body into three long drawers, above which the front of the secret well is made to simulate two smaller drawers. A simple moulding frames the base which stands on well turned ball feet. Exhibited at Carnegie Institute, Pittsburgh, Pa., in 1922.

Height, 40 *inches; width,* 36 *inches*

From the Private Collection of Miss Traver.

314 **RARE HOODED PINE SETTLE**   AMERICAN, ABOUT 1720

These great fireside settles of an early period are now rarely encountered, and especially scarce are those with the hood. The back is raked to give a comfortable sitting position. This consists of wide beaded boards, and is capped by a shallow hood with moulded edge. The bottoms of the ends are shaped to form the feet. The arms are shaped and are very unusual from the fact that they carry a bold circular frontal ornament raised some seven inches above the horizontal line of the arm. An exceedingly rare and attractive piece.

Length, 6 *feet* 3 *inches; height of back,* 51 *inches*

315 **IMPORTANT CARVED CHEST ON STAND**

AMERICAN, 17TH CENTURY

Does not Mr. Wallace Nutting make a mistake in including these carved and paneled chests in the same category with the painted ones bearing painted decorations, whereas both the type of turning and the general design of the carved pieces show them to be of earlier date? Furthermore, there are fewer examples extant. The legs upon which the body of the piece is raised are sturdy baluster form with ball feet. Crudely carved lunettes decorate the front of the single drawer, which is below two deeply moulded panels, centred by turtle back bosses. Two similar panels placed vertically one above the other appear upon the ends of the piece. Three projecting mouldings divide the piece horizontally. Constructed in oak and pine. *(From the Behrend Collection)*

Height, 32¾ *inches; width,* 24 *inches; depth,* 16 *inches*

From the Private Collection of Miss Traver.

[SEE ILLUSTRATION ON COVER]

316 **SMALL TURNED LEG AND S T R E T C H E R E D TABLE IN WALNUT AND OAK**   AMERICAN, ABOUT 1660

Was found in Virginia not far from the original Jamestown settlement. The oval top, legs and two side moulded stretchers are in Virginia walnut. The deep tool-cut lines on the vase and reel turnings of the legs show a strong English influence. The piece was no doubt made by an early settler. In original condition with the exception of slight repairs to the top and the drawer. An exceedingly rare and interesting piece.   *Height,* 26 *inches; top,* 34 x 29 *inches*

317 **MAPLE HOODED HIGHBOY WITH CLAW-AND-BALL FEET**

AMERICAN, 2ND QUARTER 18TH CENTURY

A handsomely proportioned specimen. The upper part has a well moulded broken-arch top with urn and flame finials at the sides and centre. Fitted with three small and four long drawers, the top centre drawer carved with the so-called fan or sunburst motif. The wide stiles have applied fluted pilasters. The lower part is fitted with one shallow long drawer above three small drawers, the centre one repeating the carving of the top. The shaped skirting is ornamented with pendent finials. Well curved cabriole cherry legs ending with bird-claw-and-ball feet. Original brasses. An original piece.

Height, 7 *feet; width,* 3 *feet* 4 *inches*

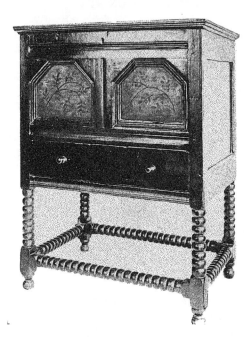

IMPORTANT CHEST ON FRAME IN OAK AND
PINE, AMERICAN, 17TH CENTURY

[NUMBER 318]

318   AN IMPORTANT CHEST ON FRAME IN OAK AND PINE

AMERICAN, 17TH CENTURY

This rare piece consists of a rectangular chest, the front of which is
divided into two canted panels decorated with painted flowers and
foliage sprays framed with mouldings.   Below is a drawer which
originally was paneled to conform to the panels above.   The ball
turned legs and stretchers of the base and deep mouldings of the rails
indicate an earlier date than other examples of the painted type.
(From the Behrend Collection)

Exhibited at Carnegie Institute, Pittsburgh, Pa., in 1922.   Illustrated
and discussed by Wallace Nutting in "Furniture of the Pilgrim Century", 1st Edition, page 96, 2nd Edition, No. 22.

Height, 35½ inches; width, 26¼ inches; depth, 18 inches
From the Private Collection of Miss Traver.

*Note: Mr. Nutting was in error when he stated in the second edi-
tion that "the drawer has since been restored with mouldings."*

68

319 LARGE JACOBEAN TAVERN TABLE AMERICAN, ABOUT 1700

The legs are of the graceful turned baluster pattern and are heavier than usual. The stretchers are of the quadrangular beaded pattern. The apron is bordered with a cross-cut four-beaded mould and has supporting brackets at its juncture with the leg-blocks. The top has framed ends and shaped vertical dove-tailed cleats which attach to the table frame with pegs, thus making the top removable. Brackets restored.

Size of top, 8 feet 2½ inches x 31 inches; height, 29½ inches

320 EARLY APPLEWOOD GUARD-ROBE

AMERICAN, EARLY 18TH CENTURY

This rare piece has something of the character of the Pennsylvania pieces of the same period, but it is credibly asserted that it was found in Connecticut. Certain minor variations such as the use of butterfly hinges for the doors and tear drop brasses on the drawers would support this assertion. The piece is constructed in two sections, the lower of which contains two drawers, while the upper is provided with double doors and shelves. Finely moulded and crowned cornice and frieze. Richly paneled stiles. The door panels are broadly chamfered and contained with early thumb-nail moulded stiles. The upper panels are finely arched. An unusual specimen and a fine one.

Height, 6 feet 6 inches; width, 4 feet 5 inches; depth, 17 inches

69

TURNED-LEG MAPLE JOINT STOOL
AMERICAN, ABOUT 1710
[NUMBER 321]

321 **TURNED-LEG MAPLE JOINT STOOL**   AMERICAN, ABOUT 1710
The legs rest upon pear-shape feet and are joined by sturdy
quadrangular stretchers. They are turned in well spaced vase and
ball forms and support a maple top with broad thumb-nail moulded
edge. These joint stools are among the rare early American pieces.
Entirely original.   *Height, 21½ inches; top,* 18 x 12 *inches*
Exhibited at Carnegie Institute, Pittsburgh, Pa., in 1922, and illustrated in "Nutting", 2nd Edition, Fig. 553.
From the Private Collection of Miss Traver.

[SEE ILLUSTRATION]

70

GROUP OF THREE RARE WEATHERVANES

TWO FORMED AS COCKS, ONE AS INDIAN

AMERICAN, 17TH, 18TH AND 19TH CENTURIES

NUMBERS 322-324

WEATHERVANES

"It was one by the village clock,
When he galloped into Lexington.
He saw the gilded weathercock
Swim in the moonlight as he passed . . *"*

—*Paul Revere's Ride.*

"Our poet left the reader to surmise that the vigilant bird atop the meeting house likewise saw Paul Revere. At the ghostly hour of one A. M., when even the young bloods of the countryside had long since called it a night, the doughty chanticleer still turned his gaze now on copse and meadowland, now on the road to Medford town. Nothing worth telling could have escaped the weathercock. And Lexington was no exception. Every village had its meeting house, and the meeting house was sure to have a weathercock patroling the highways and byways."

We are now in the midst of a weathervane revival. A rare 17th century, an 18th century, and a 19th century example are here offered.

322 **RARE WEATHERVANE COCK**   AMERICAN, LATE 17TH CENTURY

Made of copper originally gilded, traces of which can be seen through the various subsequent coats of fleck green paint. Two boldly arched flat plumes and three smaller plumes attached to his wide curved and pointed tail give a dauntless air to the one-legged, hugely spurred bird. The jaunty head has a curiously small and pointed comb, wattles, and forked beak. The slim, agile looking body has but a small raised indication of embryonic wings. Its last perch was on the Sandy Hill, Massachusetts, Meeting House, which was sold to and razed in 1848 by a Mr. John Winkley. From him the cock was purchased at that time by Mr. Aaron Morrill of Amesbury, Mass. It has been in the possession of the Morrill family since then and was recently purchased from them. The records of the Town of Amesbury show a first meeting House built in 1640 and another in 1665, in the town then known as Salisbury. The name was changed to Amesbury in 1667. In 1715 a meeting house was raised on the "Parsonage Lot" and completed in 1717. This meeting house was

71

RARE WEATHERVANE COCK
AMERICAN, LATE 17TH CENTURY
[NUMBER 322]

taken down in 1761 and rebuilt at Sandy Hill. The archaic form and design of this cock would surely justify its early attribution, and explain the numerous pilgrimages from its first perch to its final place on the spire of the Sandy Hill Meeting House, as shown in an accompanying woodcut.

Length, 30 inches; height, 20 inches; body thickness, 4 inches
From the Private Collection of Miss Traver.

[SEE ILLUSTRATION]

A WEATHERVANE COCK IN PINE
AMERICAN, 1710-40
[NUMBER 323]

323 A WEATHERVANE COCK IN PINE   AMERICAN, 1710-1740

A boldly modeled bird carved in pine, standing on and attached to a
pine ball. The legs, comb, wattles and a part of the tail are iron. It
is in the original paint of a dull greenish black hue, the wattles and
the comb in red, the ball in greenish blue. It was found in
Methuen, Massachusetts, and was probably perched on a church spire.
A research is now under way for its pedigree.

Height, including ball, 40 inches; length, 27 inches; diameter of
ball, 10 inches

From the Private Collection of Miss Traver.

[SEE ILLUSTRATION]

324 AN INDIAN WEATHERVANE IN COPPER

AMERICAN, MIDDLE 19TH CENTURY

Surmounted by an Indian standing on a bar, grasping in one hand
a bow, in the other an arrow. Modeled in copper and painted a
yellow-green.   *Height of figure, 32 inches*

73

325 ADAM CARVED PINE MANTELPIECE

ENGLISH, LAST QUARTER 18TH CENTURY

The frieze is handsomely carved in relief with festoons of flowers depending from ribbon ties, also arabesque flower scrolls and palm leaves. The cornice is moulded and dentelled. The stiles are carved with pendent husk and honeysuckle ornament. An exceptionally fine piece. *Height, 4 feet* 11 *inches; width,* 5 *feet* 7 *inches*

326 BRASS AND IRON HOB GRATE

NEW ENGLAND, LAST QUARTER 18TH CENTURY

Iron grate in architectural style with swell-front bars and deep ash tray, fluted columns at the sides. Ornamented with brass borders and ball finials. Taken from an eighteenth century house in Boston, built by Bullfinch. *Height,* 31 *inches; width,* 27 *inches*

327 PAIR OF EARLY AMERICAN BRASS ANDIRONS

Handsome pair with vase-shape pillars standing on square plinths, the tops with diamond shape knobs and flame finials. Out-curved claw-and-ball feet. *Height,* 24 *feet*

328 SMALL SERPENTINE SHAPE I R O N WIRE FENDER WITH BRASS RAIL

AMERICAN, 18TH CENTURY

Width, 35½ *inches; height,* 8 *inches*

329 COMB-BACK WINDSOR ARM ROCKER AMERICAN, 18TH CENTURY

Hooped back with seven spindles, four of which continue through the rail and are capped by a shaped top. Saddle seat, raked legs with spindle bracing and rockers.

330 FRUITWOOD TRIPOD TABLE

AMERICAN, 3RD QUARTER 18TH CENTURY

Has plain circular top, on turned vase-shape support with curved tripod legs. *Height,* 28 *inches; diameter,* 21 *inches*

331 PINE AND MAPLE CANDLESTAND AMERICAN, ABOUT 1750

Plain circular top on turned vase-shape support with boldly splayed turned tripod legs. *Height,* 24 *inches*

332 PAIR OF CHINESE PORCELAIN COCKS   KANG HSI PERIOD

Well executed figures of cocks, the bodies covered with white glaze. Standing on brown tree bases. Red combs and wattles. One slightly chipped. (*From the DeWolfe Collection*)   (2)

Height, 17½ *inches*

333 EIGHTEEN HAND PAINTED MEISSEN PLATES OF THE MARCOLINI PERIOD

Eight soup plates and ten service plates; the centres handsomely painted with clusters of fruit and flower sprays. Borders decorated with mulberry scale pattern heightened with gilt. (One slightly chipped)   (18)   *Diameter,* 9-9¾ *inches*

334 OIL PAINTING   DUTCH, 17TH CENTURY

Summer flowers, fruits and vegetables, grouped with other still life objects, forming a handsome composition. Fine coloring. Constitutes a charming decoration for an overmantel. Canvas. Gilt frame.

Size, 37½ x 54 *inches*

335 SET OF FOUR CURRIER AND IVES RACING PRINTS

"Sorrel Dan". "Lucy". "Edwin Thorn". "St. Julian". Framed.   (4)

336 SET OF FOUR CURRIER AND IVES RACING PRINTS

"Little Brown Jug". "Rowdy Boy". "Goldsmith Maid". "Hopeful". Framed.   (4)

337 SET OF FOUR CURRIER AND IVES RACING PRINTS

Famous Racehorses and their Jockeys—"Sweetser". "Maude S". "Smuggler". "Trinket".   (4)   *Size,* 17½ x 13¾ *inches*

338 SET OF FOUR CURRIER AND IVES RACING PRINTS

" h   Four". "Captain Lewis". "Edward and Swiveller". "Cling
C arly
Stone". Framed.   (4)

339 PAIR OF COLORED OLD ENGLISH SPORTING PRINTS

Race horses. "Hambletonian" and "Diamond". Mounted and framed with black and gilt glass mat.   (2)   *Size,* 26 x 21 *inches*

75